# ROUTLEDGE LIBRARY EDITIONS: LIBRARY AND INFORMATION SCIENCE

Volume 22

# COOPERATIVE COLLECTION DEVELOPMENT

# COOPERATIVE COLLECTION DEVELOPMENT
Significant Trends and Issues

Edited by
DONALD B. SIMPSON

Routledge
Taylor & Francis Group
LONDON AND NEW YORK

First published in 1998 by The Haworth Press, Inc.

This edition first published in 2020
by Routledge
2 Park Square, Milton Park, Abingdon, Oxon OX14 4RN

and by Routledge
52 Vanderbilt Avenue, New York, NY 10017

*Routledge is an imprint of the Taylor & Francis Group, an informa business*

© 1998 The Haworth Press, Inc.

All rights reserved. No part of this book may be reprinted or reproduced or utilised in any form or by any electronic, mechanical, or other means, now known or hereafter invented, including photocopying and recording, or in any information storage or retrieval system, without permission in writing from the publishers.

*Trademark notice*: Product or corporate names may be trademarks or registered trademarks, and are used only for identification and explanation without intent to infringe.

*British Library Cataloguing in Publication Data*
A catalogue record for this book is available from the British Library

ISBN: 978-0-367-34616-4 (Set)
ISBN: 978-0-429-34352-0 (Set) (ebk)
ISBN: 978-0-367-36947-7 (Volume 22) (hbk)
ISBN: 978-0-367-36948-4 (Volume 22) (pbk)
ISBN: 978-0-429-35201-0 (Volume 22) (ebk)

**Publisher's Note**
The publisher has gone to great lengths to ensure the quality of this reprint but points out that some imperfections in the original copies may be apparent.

**Disclaimer**
The publisher has made every effort to trace copyright holders and would welcome correspondence from those they have been unable to trace.

# Cooperative Collection Development: Significant Trends and Issues

Donald B. Simpson
Editor

*Cooperative Collection Development: Significant Trends and Issues* has been co-published simultaneously as *Collection Management*, Volume 23, Number 4 1998.

The Haworth Press, Inc.
New York • London

*Cooperative Collection Development: Significant Trends and Issues* has been co-published simultaneously as *Collection Management*™, Volume 23, Number 4 1998.

© 1998 by The Haworth Press, Inc. All rights reserved. No part of this work may be reproduced or utilized in any form or by any means, electronic or mechanical, including photocopying, microfilm and recording, or by any information storage and retrieval system, without permission in writing from the publisher. Printed in the United States of America.

The development, preparation, and publication of this work has been undertaken with great care. However, the publisher, employees, editors, and agents of The Haworth Press and all imprints of The Haworth Press, Inc., including The Haworth Medical Press® and Pharmaceutical Products Press®, are not responsible for any errors contained herein or for consequences that may ensue from use of materials or information contained in this work. Opinions expressed by the author(s) are not necessarily those of The Haworth Press, Inc.

Cover design by Thomas J. Mayshock Jr.

**Library of Congress Cataloging-in-Publication Data**

Cooperative collection development : significant trends and issues / Donald B. Simpson, editor.
    p. cm.
    "Has been co-published simultaneously as Collection management, volume 23, number 4, 1998."
    Includes bibliographical references and index.
    ISBN 0-7890-0688-X (alk. paper)
    1. Research libraries-Collection development-United States. 2. Library cooperation-United States. I. Simpson, Donald B. II. Collection management.
Z675.R45C67 1998
025.2'1-dc21
                                                                                          98-32066
                                                                                              CIP

# Cooperative Collection Development: Significant Trends and Issues

## CONTENTS

| | |
|---|---|
| Preface | xi |
| Shifting Boundaries: Managing Research Library Collections at the Beginning of the Twenty-First Century<br>*Joseph J. Branin* | 1 |
| Cooperative Collection Development: Yesterday, Today, and Tomorrow<br>*Robert P. Holley* | 19 |
| The Center for Research Libraries and Cooperative Collection Development: Partnerships in Progress<br>*Gay N. Dannelly* | 37 |
| The Role of the Center for Research Libraries in the History and Future of Cooperative Collection Development<br>*Linda A. Naru* | 47 |
| Cooperative Collection Management: Online Discussion<br>*Milton T. Wolf* | 59 |
| Index | 95 |

# Preface

The art of cooperation requires librarians' ability to comprehend and support "big picture" goals and the skills to incorporate "common good" objectives into local activities so that there is constructive and affirmative benefit to one's own programs and services.

Interlibrary cooperation is a strong historical theme. European universities began international exchange programs in the early 1800s. Union catalogs and interlibrary loan were resource sharing conventions beginning in the early 1900s.

Some of the most famous and some of the successful cooperative collection development programs arose, ironically, in the development of very large research collections: after World War II, when U.S. university library collections grew rapidly, librarians concluded that, realistically, they could not all obtain all foreign publications. The Farmington Plan (ca. 1948-1972) was designed to meet the challenge of increasing publishing production: collecting responsibility was distributed among university and research libraries, thereby achieving full coverage of these materials. The goal of the Foreign Newspaper Microfilm Project of the Association for Research Libraries was to cover much of the acquisition and preservation of newspapers. The Midwest Inter-Library Center (MILC, later the Center for Research Libraries) was organized as a storage library and an active acquisitions program for foreign publications.

There is a broad compass of cooperative collection development efforts in place today. At one end of the scale is the passive strategy where a selector knows other libraries' policies and relies on these libraries to continue collecting practices and to offer ongoing opportunities to use collections through interlibrary loan. On the other end are formal, contractual arrangements to participate in well-defined cooperative programs such as regional efforts such as the Boston Library Consortium, statewide consortia like OhioLINK, and international organizations such as the Research Libraries Group and the Center for Research Libraries.

Cooperative collection development in theory and practice has significant impact on general collection development as well as on resource sharing, public services, and the goal of universal access to publications. Cooperative collection development's ultimate objective is to maximize the library materials to which researchers have access while minimizing local budget expenditures.

Few would dispute that these goals and objectives of cooperative collection development are good ideas. However, the measures of the impacts of such programs, the extent of the value that cooperative collection development contributes to libraries, and ways to improve and increase the benefits of such programs must be seriously considered and debated.

Cooperation underlies some of the compelling developments, trends, and realities affecting research libraries today: budget demands of electronic resources; serving remote users; preserving printed works and electronic media; supporting interdisciplinary collection development; balancing access and ownership; library materials price increases. This volume focuses on these themes.

*Donald B. Simpson*

# Shifting Boundaries:
# Managing Research Library Collections at the Beginning of the Twenty-First Century

Joseph J. Branin

**SUMMARY.** In this paper I would like to take the reader on a whirlwind review of collection management practices and issues in research libraries in the United States. Although I will greatly compress and oversimplify the contemporary history of collection management, the brevity is not as extreme as it may at first appear, for it was not until the 1950s that collection development in the United States began to emerge as a coherent management science. Over a period of about thirty-five years, from roughly 1950 through the mid-1980s, collection building in research libraries in the United States was professionalized and codified. In the first part of this paper I will review three significant issues–the rapid expansion of education, scholarship, and library collections; the shift from collection development to collection management; and attempts at cooperative collection development–that influenced the evolution of collection management during this formative period. *[Article copies available for a fee from The Haworth Document Delivery Service: 1-800-342-9678. E-mail address: getinfo@haworthpressinc.com]*

---

Joseph J. Branin is Dean of Libraries, State University of New York at Stony Brook, Stony Brook, NY 11794-3300 (e-mail: Jbranin@ccmail.sunysb.edu).

A version of this paper was presented at the Research Libraries Group (RLG) and Council of University Research Libraries (CURL) Symposium on "Local Access to Global Collections," University College, London, on September 23, 1996.

[Haworth co-indexing entry note]: "Shifting Boundaries: Managing Research Library Collections at the Beginning of the Twenty-First Century." Branin, Joseph J. Co-published simultaneously in *Collection Management* (The Haworth Press, Inc.) Vol. 23, No. 4, 1998, pp. 1-17; and: *Cooperative Collection Development: Significant Trends and Issues* (ed: Donald B. Simpson) The Haworth Press, Inc., 1998, pp. 1-17. Single or multiple copies of this article are available for a fee from The Haworth Document Delivery Service [1-800-342-9678, 9:00 a.m. - 5:00 p.m. (EST). E-mail address: getinfo@haworthpressinc.com].

© 1998 by The Haworth Press, Inc. All rights reserved.

## INTRODUCTION: PAST, PRESENT, AND FUTURE OF COLLECTION MANAGEMENT

During the last decade, from the mid-1980s to the present, the new science of collection management has had little chance to form a solid core of practice or tradition because current economic and technological changes have quickly modified or even reversed recently established ideas about how best to operate collection management programs. In the second part of this paper I will examine the most important challenges–a weak library economy, a new digital information system, and pervasive change–facing collection management librarians during the last ten years. Finally, based on lessons learned from the last half of the twentieth century, I will make some predictions about what collection management will look like at the beginning of the twenty-first century, when I believe research librarians will truly be engaged by the theme of local access to global collections.

## THE FORMATIVE YEARS OF COLLECTION MANAGEMENT: 1950-1985

The contemporary history of collection management in research libraries in the United States began in the 1950s as America emerged from World War II as a preeminent world power. For the next thirty-five years, the rapid expansion of education, scholarship, publications, and library collections in the United States–an expansion often called "the information explosion"–created great optimism and innovation in research librarianship. Librarians found themselves managing large sums of money and rapidly expanding collections in not just a few prestigious or national libraries but in literally hundreds of emerging research libraries scattered across the country. With their ranks increasing and their libraries growing, research librarians began to feel the need to examine their acquisition efforts and to begin codifying and organizing their collection building activities. There was a call in research librarianship to move from just "developing" or acquiring collections to more scientifically "managing" them.[1]

The ensuing systematic reflection on collection development and management led to some interesting findings about how collections were being used by scholars and students, about how much these collections cost to acquire and manage over time, and about how to coordinate local collection building with regional and national cooperative collection development programs.[2] As librarians during this period struggled nobly to manage the print information explosion, another challenge in the form of a whole new information technology based on the computer was quietly but quickly gathering strength. By the mid-1980s, the information explosion had turned into a real information revolution.

## *Rapid Expansion of Research Libraries*

One has only to talk with or read about research librarians whose careers spanned the pre- and post-1950 worlds to get an indication of how the scope of scholarship in the United States changed radically in a very brief period of time. Before World War II, librarians such as James Skipper, a former director of the Research Libraries Group, could observe that library service to scholarship and research was "reasonably adequate." Study in this country concentrated on Western culture and the classical areas of science. However, as the United States emerged as a world power at mid-century, it came to require "detailed knowledge of areas of the world, which were little more than geographical expressions several generations ago."[3] Edward Holley, Professor and former Dean of the School of Library Science at the University of North Carolina, noted the same historic expansion of the scope of research libraries' collection interests. Before the war, American "collection efforts had been primarily Western European in orientation." But after 1945, the country's libraries expanded their collecting scope to include Africa, the Middle East, Asia, and Eastern Europe, especially the former Soviet Union.[4] By mid-century and during the Cold War period, detailed knowledge of all areas of the world and the rapid growth of applied and specialized science marked the patterns of scholarship in the United States.

The rapid growth of U.S. research library collections in size, variety of formats, and breadth of subject coverage was simply amazing between 1950 and the mid-1980s. For example, the University of California, Berkeley, Library's manuscript collection increased from 4.5 million to 35 million papers between 1963 and 1984.[5] In 1986, Paul Mosher, now Dean of Libraries at the University of Pennsylvania and one of the leaders of the collection management movement, could estimate that more than 70 million titles had already been published and about 700,000 new titles were appearing each year.[6] Recent UNESCO statistics estimate that worldwide annual book publishing was at 715,500 titles in 1980 and 842,000 in 1989.[7] Librarians were–and, of course, still are–drowning in an ocean of print information. Libraries, even in the best of times, could not keep up with this explosive growth in information. The example I often use to illustrate this point is the library building situation at Columbia University in New York City, where two landmark buildings, the Low and Butler Libraries, were built to house what architects at the time (in 1894 and in 1934) thought was needed for collections. Both buildings ran out of collection storage space quickly.

## *From Collection Development to Collection Management*

By the end of the 1970s, collection management as a discipline was beginning to mature. Selection of material for acquisitions had shifted from the teaching faculty to librarians, and a number of libraries had appointed full-time collection development officers and subject bibliographers to shape and manage their rapidly growing collections.[8] In 1979 Allen Kent's seminal and controversial work entitled *Use of Library Materials: The University of Pittsburgh Study* appeared. Kent and his research team carefully studied the use of the library collection at the University of Pittsburgh over a seven-year period and concluded "that any given book purchased had only slightly better than one chance in two of ever being borrowed." As books on the shelves aged and did not circulate, their likelihood of ever circulating diminished to as low as one chance in fifty. Journal use, in general, was also discovered to be low.[9]

Also in 1979, Charles Osburn issued his study, *Academic Research and Library Resources: Changing Patterns in America,* which in my opinion is the single most important work of the collection management movement. In it Osburn identified a number of significant trends in scholarship that were changing the nature of research and publication in the United States. Massive infusions of federal money for research, the predominance of the sciences, and the decline in foreign language competencies were, according to Osburn, changing the patterns of usefulness of library resources. The humanities-based model of collection development, with its emphasis on a well-rounded and complete record of scholarship, which Osburn found dominant in most libraries up to that time, was creating more and more frustration for both users and librarians. The new patterns of scholarship and library use, instead, called for a more service-oriented model of collection development, where currency, responsiveness, and focused attention to the needs of users were emphasized.[10]

These findings and ideas were communicated to the library profession through a series of regional collection management institutes sponsored by the American Library Association during the decade of the 1980s. At the very first institute held at Stanford University in 1981, Paul Mosher gave a keynote address entitled "Fighting Back: From Collection Development to Collection Management."[11] In it he outlined the major tasks of the new discipline of "collection management." Collection management was more than just the development or building of collections and more than just the selection and acquisitions of library resources. Collection management included these activities, but it also encompassed collection policy preparation, bibliographer training, collection analysis and use studies, preservation, and above all cooperative collection development. No library could be self-sufficient in an age that produced so much information. An organized network of local, regional, and national cooperative collection management programs was needed among research libraries to ensure that the comprehensive record of scholarship was acquired, organized, and preserved.

## *Attempts at Cooperative Collection Development*

What emerged over this thirty-five year period was a two-stage plan for collection management. In the words of Charles Osburn, collection managers had two broad goals: first, "service to the identifiable needs of the immediate constituency," and second, "integration of local development into the national system of resource sharing in support of the long-range national academic research effort."[12] The second of these goals can be labeled "cooperative collection development," and many such efforts were undertaken in the U.S. between 1950 and 1986. Some notable examples include the Farmington Plan to distribute national responsibility for foreign acquisitions, the ill-fated National Periodicals Center, the Center for Research Libraries, the Conspectus efforts of the Research Libraries Group (RLG), and many local and regional cooperative efforts such as the Research Triangle

Libraries program in North Carolina.[13] These cooperative efforts produced mixed results. By and large, there was more planning and discussion than successful, sustained implementation. Large-scale coordinated efforts especially proved hard to sustain, and by the end of the 1980s cooperative collection development on a national level had lost much of its luster.

## CURRENT TRENDS AND PRACTICE IN COLLECTION MANAGEMENT, 1986-1998

Over the last decade, collection management, like all other areas of librarianship in the United States, has been dominated by two trends: economic downsizing and the revolution in digital information technology. These forces have brought substantial change to the organization of libraries and their operational practices, in many ways shaking libraries to their very core.

### *Economic Decline*

The economic trend, which is one of a weakening library economy in the United States, is all too easy to document. Association of Research Libraries (ARL) statistics, for example, as seen in Chart 1, show an 8% decline in serials purchased and a 23% decline in monographs purchased between 1986 and 1995 by major research libraries in North America.[14]

This decline has been further documented and analyzed in a number of recent national studies such as the 1992 Mellon Foundation report entitled *University Libraries and Scholarly Communication* and the 1994 *Project Reports of the AAU/ARL Task Forces*.[15] Chart 2, which is from the *Project Reports of the AAU/ARL Task Forces*, illustrates, through OCLC cataloging data, the dramatic decline in foreign acquisitions by U.S. libraries since 1988.[16]

The downsizing in research libraries is not confined to just new collection acquisitions. In fact, libraries in general have maintained healthier collection budgets than personnel budgets. Chart 3, taken from the Mellon Foundation Study, *University Libraries and Scholarly Communication*, shows the changing percentages of the components of research library expenditures from 1963 to 1991.[17] Salary expenditures as a percentage of the total library budget have shown a

CHART 1. Monograph and Serial Costs in ARL Libraries, 1986-1995

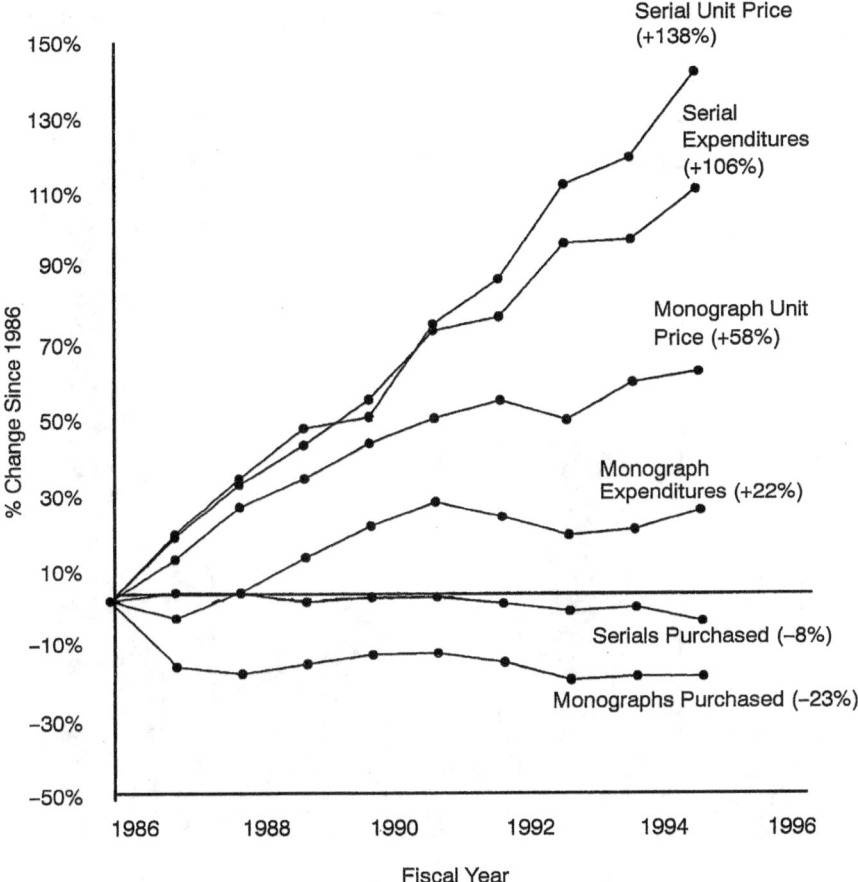

Source: *ARL Statistics 1994-95*, Copyright 1996 by the Association of Research Libraries, Washington, DC. Used by permission.

steady decline, while operating expenditures have risen, and acquisitions expenditures have remained relatively flat.

Staff size is shrinking, and libraries are scrambling to find new organizational models usually based on concepts of downsizing, flattening the hierarchy, more flexible work units, and a team approach to management and supervision. For collection management this has

8  *Cooperative Collection Development: Significant Trends and Issues*

CHART 2. Trends in Foreign Acquisitions

BASED ON OCLC DATABASE
1992 DATA LOW DUE TO CATALOGING BACKLOGS

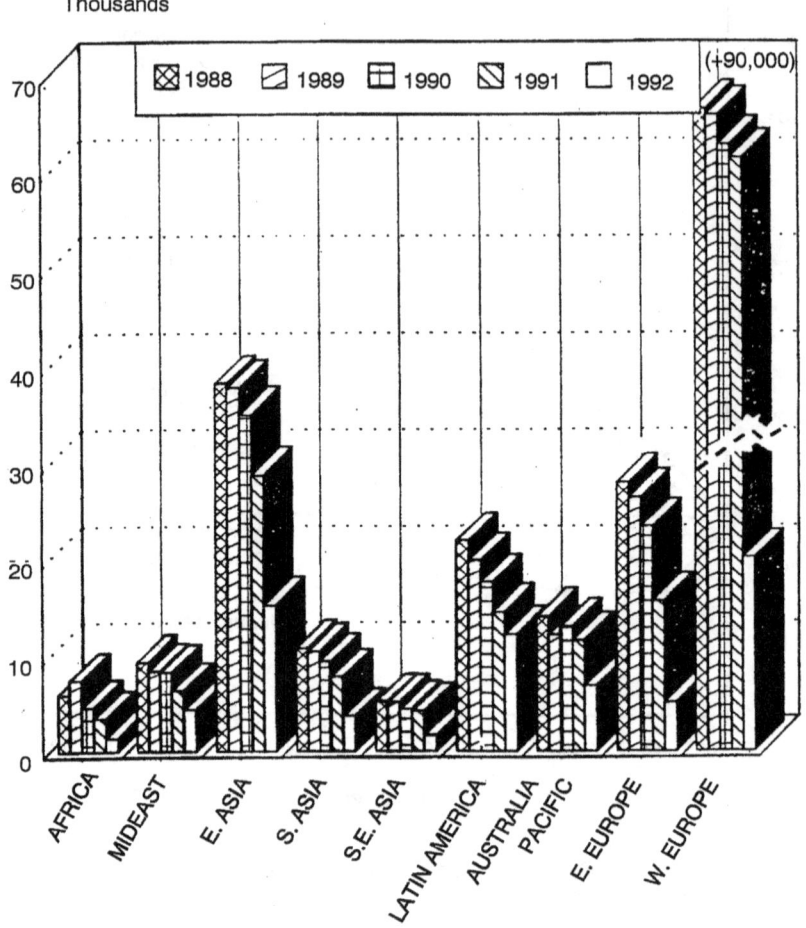

Source: Report of the AAU Task Force on Acquisition and Distribution of Foreign Language and Area Studies Materials, *Association of America Universities Research Libraries Project: Report of the AAU Task Forces*. Copyright 1994 by the Association of Research Libraries, Washington, DC. Used by permission.

CHART 3. Components of Library Budget (Percentage Shares), All-24 Universities 1963, 1970, 1982, and 1991

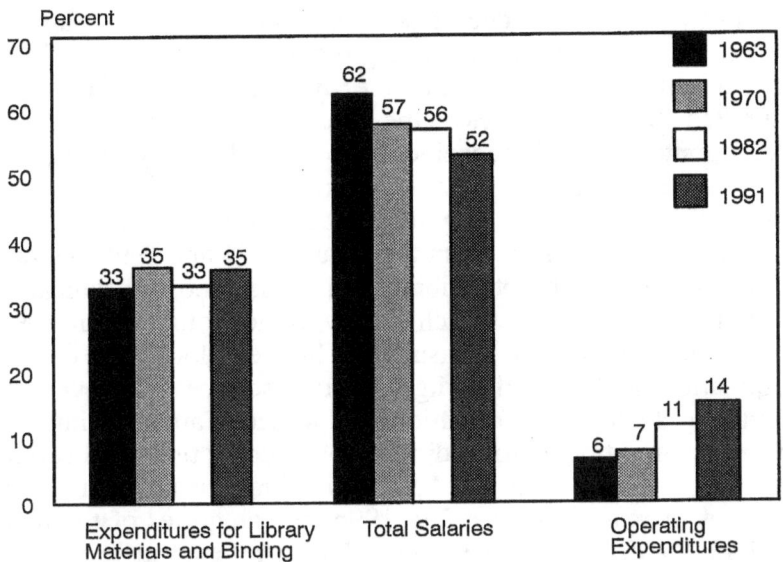

meant a loss of specialty, a loss of full-time jobs in collection management, and the outsourcing of many collection management activities through the use of approval plans, aggregate electronic collections, and collection analysis and preservation done by outside vendors.

## *Digital Information System*

The last decade has certainly been marked by the introduction of digital information services in research libraries. Librarians now have two information systems, one print and one electronic, to manage. As digital information sources were first introduced in research libraries, there was a good deal of conflict with the traditional information system: what might be called the cultural wars between print and electronic proponents began. For a taste of these print versus digital cultural wars in libraries one can read Nicholson Baker's pieces in *The New Yorker* on the demise of the card catalog and controversy over the new San Francisco Public Library building.[18] These battles have now eased or ceased in most libraries, but there are still tensions over priorities, allocations, and the desires of different constituency groups of library users. In some libraries, collection development staff and bibliographers came late to digital resources, and as a result, they let other parts of the organization–administration, systems, or reference–take on the responsibility for selection decisions regarding electronic databases.

The digital information system is growing faster than most librarians would have predicted. For example, by January of 1996 there were an estimated 90,000 Web sites on the Internet, and according to Nicholas Negroponte in *Wired* magazine, the Web is doubling in size every fifty days with a homepage added every four seconds.[19]

Despite this phenomenal growth, print resources still largely dominate research libraries. Data from the annual 1995 and 1996 budgets at the University of Minnesota Library, which is probably typical of a large publicly supported research library, indicate that about 10% of that library's total effort, as measured by budget allocations, goes into the acquisitions and support of digital library services. However, commitments to electronic information and services are growing much faster than commitments to traditional print collections and services. Again using the University of Minnesota Library as an example, percentages of increase from 1995 to 1996 for categories of the budget were 21.1% for database acquisitions, 6.4% for print acquisitions, 28.3% for electronic support services, and 11.2% for print support services (see Chart 4). At the University of Minnesota, where print still dominates,

CHART 4. Growth of Networked Services

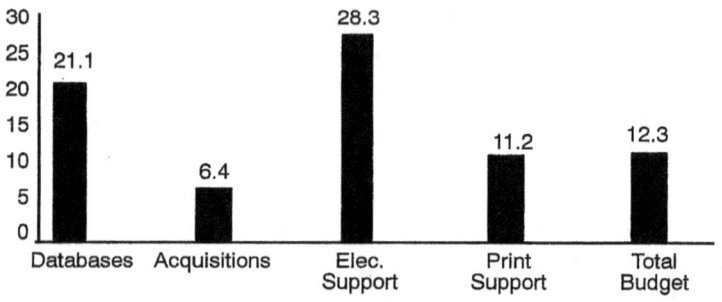

Percent of Increase by Budget Category, 1995 to 1996, University of Minnesota Libraries

commitments to electronic resources and services are growing twice as fast as print support.

## Coping with Substantial Change

Collection management librarians are faced with a very changeable environment at the end of the twentieth century. Selectors and bibliographers are trying to do their work with less buying power than they had a decade ago. There are fewer staff in collection management, and many selectors and bibliographers work at collection management part-time and handle a much broader range of discipline responsibilities. The digital information system is truly revolutionizing the way scholarly information is published, organized, and maintained. The scope and amount of all this change is difficult to comprehend and manage. As librarians I think it is in our nature to want to cope with change in a rational and scientific manner; however, what may be called for today is a more radical approach to facing change, an approach that might be called "upside-down thinking," an approach to our changeable environment that is more "unreasonable" and creative.[20]

I do predict that we will see some "upside-down" changes in collection management in the first years of the new century ahead. In the last fifty years, local print collection management has dominated our work. Cooperative collection development and resource sharing, that is more global perspectives, have played only minor–and some might say problematic–roles in our work as collection management librarians. But in the near future, access to remote provision centers, whether they are print archives or centralized electronic data banks, will become much more important. Local collections will lose their supremacy as digital information systems make physical location of information sources less and less important. As the new century begins, we will be concerned more and more with what might be called "local access to global collections."

## LOCAL AND GLOBAL COLLECTION MANAGEMENT AT THE BEGINNING OF THE TWENTY-FIRST CENTURY

I would like to end this review of collection management trends in the United States with some predictions about what will happen in this field in the next ten to twenty years. In my cloudy crystal ball, I can foresee four important trends: first, radical changes in the very structure of information services and scholarly communications; second, local print collections losing their supremacy in our library work and services; third, the creation of provision centers to serve specialized, regional, or national collection needs; and finally, fourth, the new challenge of managing local access to global collections.

## *Changing Structure of Scholarly Communication*

We can already see some of the changes that are beginning to reshape the structure of scholarly communication. Early forms of Internet publishing that by-pass traditional publishers and libraries are exemplified by projects like the E-Print Archive at Los Alamos National Laboratory. Paul Ginsparg, the physicist who pioneered the E-Print Archive, claims that the potential of the Internet will free scholars from the tyranny of traditional publishing.[21] Costs will be lower, access will be faster, and authors will have more control over their own work in the new networked environment. On the other hand, the digital information system may foster more publisher control over scholarly information. Reed Elsevier, for example, has been aggressively consolidating its control over specialized scientific journals, and its online services may not be cheaper or less restrictive.[22] Information service vendors such as the Online Computer Library Center (OCLC), the Research Libraries Group (RLG), University Microfilms International (UMI), the Institute for Scientific Information (ISI), the Information Access Company (IAC), and Ovid are moving quickly to become "aggregators" of digital collections and services. These aggregate digital collections integrate catalogs and indexes with full-text electronic documents and with document delivery services. Scholarly societies, university presses, and commercial publishers are also beginning to offer and package their publications in digital form. Johns Hopkins University's Project Muse is a good example of a university press moving from print to electronic distribution of its publication. Project Muse (http://muse.jhu.edu/muse.html) provides networked subscription access to the full text of Johns Hopkins University Press's forty-plus list of scholarly journals in humanities, social sciences, and mathematics. High Wire Press (http://www-jbe.stanford.edu), the Internet imprint of Stanford University Libraries, is another interesting example of innovation in scholarly publishing. High Wire Press has a growing list of online journals in biology, medicine, and general science. Elsevier, Academic Press, and the American Chemical Society now all market their entire line of electronic journals as a complete package to individual libraries, local library consortia, and even statewide or region-wide groups of libraries.

It is not just the format that is changing as authors and publishers adopt new digital technology. Control of publishing is changing; distribution means are being altered; and ownership rights to information are being questioned and revised. The very basic structures and tenets of the scholarly record–authorship, the framing devices of the book and journal–are giving way to new concepts of bibliographic control and organization. Ross Atkinson in his insightful article "Networks, Hypertext, and Academic Information Services: Some Longer-Range Implications" predicts the design of new document structures that may "represent fundamental revisions in the very modality of communications" and that "may affect and alter some of our basic assumptions about the nature of information itself."[23] The ability to use hyperlinks to integrate scholarship online is an extraordinary driving force for the adoption of the new digital information system, a force with which the print format cannot compete.

## *Local Print Collections Lose Supremacy*

When one looks at the historical context of collection management, it is clear that local print collection development has been the dominant concern of research librarians during the second half of the twentieth century. For all our talk and plans about our global responsibilities to take a coordinated and cooperative approach to collecting and preserving the comprehensive record of scholarship, our real priorities and limited resources have been focused on local collections that meet local needs. The traditional print format of most scholarly information is not easy to share, and our faculty and students–and library staffs too–have demanded strong local collections.

But the digital information system is changing all these geographic or information boundary issues. The early management of electronic databases in libraries provides a good example of this change. At first libraries offered electronic databases locally by purchasing, mounting, and providing stand-alone or local networking of CD-ROMs and magnetic tape files. However, now with the Internet, client-server architecture, and centralized database management, we prefer to let others manage our electronic provision sources, while we manage local access. If we can network reliably and economically over the Internet to a remote server that can send us the information we need, then we only have to worry about the local or client access and not the remote server provision. As it becomes easier and more economical to move print information around through faxing, digital conversion, and better surface delivery systems, we will see more centralized document delivery service options for print information as well. Centralized provision centers–both digital and print provision centers–with highly distributed access through either electronic networks or print document delivery systems will likely increase as a preferred pattern for organizing information services in the twenty-first century.

Certainly many research librarians are questioning the economic sense of trying to maintain large local collections to all or most scientific and technical journals. The costs have simply climbed too fast, and most research libraries have now gone through several rounds of journal cancellations. Document delivery services are becoming more effective, and for certain journal titles, where use is below a certain threshold, per use access through print or electronic document delivery makes more sense than does local ownership. In 1991 and 1992, staff at the State University of New York at Albany gathered data on the use of their journal collection.[24] In the sciences they found that of the 1,403 current journal titles in their collection, 299 could be described as "low use" titles, that is, titles for which there were five or fewer uses in a year. These 229 low use titles were tracked as having 522 uses during the year. Their total subscription cost to the library was $103,758; therefore, cost per use–and this excludes any overhead cost for processing, managing, and storing these titles–was $198.77.

Vendors and publishers from the commercial and non-profit sectors are rushing to meet the market demand for effective print document delivery services and electronic distribution of full-text collections of current literature, government reports, journal articles, and even backruns of journals. In just a matter of a few short years, significant amounts of scholarly content have become available in digital form, and as this new digital information system matures, libraries will spend increasing amounts of their budgets on access to electronic sources rather than on local ownership of information resources. I do believe, however, that the print information system will remain with us and be a significant part of our library services into the foreseeable future. We will have to manage two information systems, but the trend in both systems will be towards centralized provision and distributed access. Library provision from central data banks and from regional or national archive storage centers will become more commonplace.[25]

## *Creation of Provision Centers*

The old models for global provision will not work in the new environment of the twenty-first century. The highly distributed provision and voluntary resource sharing system of interlibrary loan is breaking down under the growing traffic, high costs, and inefficiencies of a system that was designed for marginal, specialized, and complementary services. Today, access to rather than ownership of information is becoming a more central activity of research libraries, and provision centers are springing up to fill this need. Provision centers are libraries or commercial organizations that have strong collections, effective bibliographic access to these collections, rapid delivery services, and a business goal of making money through marketing, guaranteed turn around times, and competitive pricing. You can see these provision centers beginning to emerge in services offered by such organizations as CARL Uncover, the British Library Document Supply Centre, the Canadian Institute for Scientific and Technical Information (CISTI), the Institute for Scientific Information (ISI), and the Linda Hall Library.

These provision centers will be the source of first resort for high-volume document delivery sources. Their economies of scale will make them more competitive and efficient than small interlibrary loan departments. They will operate on a marketplace basis, receiving fees for their services and paying copyright owners royalty fees for copying. These provision centers, of course, will not have all needed sources of information, so I expect some form of more specialized interlibrary loan to continue among research libraries.

## *Managing Local Access to Global Collections*

In the past, local collection development has occupied the self-interest of research librarians. Our constituents and our own values have centered on strong local print collections. However, I predict a reversal of roles as the new digital information system matures and as provision centers become better at print document delivery services. Local access, not local collections, will be the most important goal. It will be in our self-interest to take a global perspective to collections or provision, whether electronic or print. It will be more cost and service effective to rely on remote centralized provision centers for many of our library services. Our jobs as knowledge management librarians will be to create the right mix of local and remote provision and to ensure that local access to global collections is well organized. We will have increasing responsibility to see that unique local collections, what we now call special collections, become part of the global scholarly record through better bibliographic control and new forms of publication and access.

## NOTES

1. Joseph J. Branin, editor. *Collection Management in the 1990s* (Chicago: American Library Association, 1993) ix-xii.

2. See Allen Kent et al., *Use of Library Materials: The University of Pittsburgh Study* (New York: Marcel Dekker, 1979); Charles B. Osburn, *Academic Research and Library Resources: Changing Patterns in America* (Westport, CT: Greenwood Press, 1979); and Paul H. Mosher and Marcia Pankake, "A Guide to Coordinated and Cooperative Collection Development," *Library Resources and Technical Services* 27 (October/December 1983), 417-420.

3. James E. Skipper, "National Planning for Research Development," *Library Trends* 15 (October 1966), 321.

4. Edward G. Holley, "North American Efforts at Worldwide Acquisitions Since 1945," *Collection Management* 9 (Summer / Fall 1987): 92.

5. University of California, Berkeley, General Library, "Estelle Rebec Retires," *CU News* 39 (August 2, 1984), 1.

6. Paul H. Mosher, "A National Scheme For Collaboration in Collection Development: The RLG-NCIP Effort," in *Coordinating Cooperative Collection Development: A National Perspective*, ed. Wilson Luquire (New York: The Haworth Press, Inc., 1986), 21.

7. UNESCO publishing statistics

8. Ross Atkinson, "Old Forms, New Forms: The Challenge of Collection Development," *College and Research Libraries* 50 (September 1989).

9. Allen Kent et al., *Use of Library materials: The University of Pittsburgh Study* (New York: Marcel Dekker, 1979), 10.

10. Charles B. Osburn, *Academic Research and Library Resources: Changing Patterns in America* (Westport, CT: Greenwood Press, 1979).

11. *Collection Management for the 1990s*, ix-xii.

12. Osburn, p. 140.

13. Joseph J. Branin, "Cooperative Collection Development," in *Collection Management: A New Treatise*, eds. Charles B. Osburn and Ross Atkinson (Greenwich, CT: JAI Press, 1991), 81-110.

14. Association of Research Libraries, *ARL Statistics: 194-95* (Washington, D.C.: Association of Research Libraries, 1996), 10.

15. Anthony M. Cummings et al., *University Libraries and Scholarly Communications: Study Prepared for the Andrew W. Mellon Foundation* (Washington, D.C.: Association of Research Libraries, 1992) and Association of American Universities and Association of American University Research Libraries, *Project Reports of the AAU Task Forces* (Washington, D.C.: Association of Research Libraries, 1994).

16. *Project Reports of the AAU Task Forces*, p. 15.

17. *University Libraries and Scholarly Communication*, p. 47.

18. See Nicholson Baker, "Discards," *The New Yorker* 70 (October 14, 1994), 64-70+, and "The Author vs. the Library," *The New Yorker* 72 (October 14, 1996), 50-53+.

19. Nicholas Negroponte, Wired Magazine, 2-1-96, also Web statistics net.genesis

20. Joseph J. Branin, editor. *Managing Change in Academic Libraries*. (New York: The Haworth Press, Inc., 1996), 1-6.

21. Paul Ginsparg, "Winners and Losers in the Global Village," *http://xxx.lanl.gov/blurb/pg96usesco.html.*

22. Kenneth N. Gilpin, "Concerns About an Aggressive Publishing Giant," *New York Times*, December 29, 1997, D2.

23. Ross Atkinson, "Networks, Hypertext, and Academic Information Services: Some Longer-Range Implications," *College and Research Libraries*, 54 (May 1993), 211.

24. Eleanor A. Gossen and Suzanne Irving, "Ownership Versus Access and Low-Use Periodical Titles," *Library Resources & Technical Services*, 39 January 1995, 43-52.

25. Jeffrey R. Young, "In the New Model for the Research Library, Unused Books Are Out, Computers Are In," *The Chronicle of Higher Education*, October 17, 1997, A27-28.

# Cooperative Collection Development: Yesterday, Today, and Tomorrow

Robert P. Holley

**SUMMARY.** This article evaluates the past, present, and future of cooperative collection development (CCD) from the perspective of a faculty member in library and information science education. The first section gives assumptions about the nature of CCD prior to arrival of the Internet, including the various forms of CCD activities and the inherent administrative and financial costs associated with implementation. Formal CCD may not have been a cost-effective way of increasing the storehouse of available research materials. The article next discusses the positive and negative consequences of the Internet for CCD. While email, file transfer, and digitization are simplifying document delivery, reliance on the Internet may lead to less attention to traditional CCD and to a devaluing of print formats. While the future of CCD is murky, individual research libraries, except for the very largest, may have a lesser role to play. The future of CCD may lie in providing financial subsidies to fund large storehouses of digital records. *[Article copies available for a fee from The Haworth Document Delivery Service: 1-800-342-9678. E-mail address: getinfo@haworthpressinc.com]*

## INTRODUCTION AND QUALIFICATIONS

I have been asked to consider cooperative collection development from the perspective of a faculty member in library and information science. I will first, however, present my background to give my credentials and to help readers understand how I arrived at my views.

---

Robert P. Holley is Director, Library and Information Science Program, Wayne State University, Detroit, MI.

[Haworth co-indexing entry note]: "Cooperative Collection Development: Yesterday, Today, and Tomorrow." Holley, Robert P. Co-published simultaneously in *Collection Management* (The Haworth Press, Inc.) Vol. 23, No. 4, 1998, pp. 19-35; and: *Cooperative Collection Development: Significant Trends and Issues* (ed: Donald B. Simpson) The Haworth Press, Inc., 1998, pp. 19-35. Single or multiple copies of this article are available for a fee from The Haworth Document Delivery Service [1-800-342-9678, 9:00 a.m. - 5:00 p.m. (EST). E-mail address: getinfo@haworthpressinc.com].

© 1998 by The Haworth Press, Inc. All rights reserved.

I have been chief collection development officer at two ARL libraries. I became Assistant Director for Technical Services at the Marriott Library, University of Utah, in 1980 and stayed until 1988. The Marriott Library provided library service for all disciplines on campus except law and medicine that were administratively separate. Because of the relative geographic isolation, Utah academic libraries had developed a strong tradition of cooperative collection development under the auspices of the Utah College Library Council (UCLC). Collection development representatives met regularly from the University of Utah; Brigham Young University, Utah's other ARL library; Utah State University; and Weber State College. The group coordinated major purchases such as microform sets as well as designating subject areas where one institution would have primary responsibility. The libraries encouraged access and use by the students and faculty of the other institutions.

I moved to Wayne State University, Detroit, Michigan in 1988 to become Associate Dean of University Libraries. While this position included responsibilities as chief collection development officer, I had much less hands-on experience because day-to-day collection development decisions resided at the unit level in the four major libraries (Humanities/Social Sciences, Science, Law, and Medicine). My role was to work with unit directors on general policies, to allocate the budget in consultation with the Dean, and to coordinate major purchases and the expenditure of special year end funds that had become the practice at Wayne State University.

Unlike Utah, Michigan did not have a history of cooperation in higher education. The three major universities (University of Michigan, Michigan State University, and Wayne State University) are constitutionally independent with relatively little oversight power given to any governmental body. Since competition for students is fierce, the availability of library resources for students from other institutions has been a thorny issue since access to an extensive collection is a recruitment advantage for the larger universities. As representative of the Dean, I often attended meetings of the Council of Library Deans and Directors where the library directors from the fifteen state-supported colleges and universities met to discuss common concerns including cooperative collection development and resource sharing. Even after commissioning a consultant to examine ways to implement closer cooperation, the group never could resolve the issues of resource sharing, a necessary precondition for cooperative collection development. The three Michigan ARL libraries–Michigan State University, the University of Michigan, and Wayne State University–were more successful in this area with the formation of the Michigan Research Libraries Triangle (MRLT) in 1991. Cooperative collection development was a high priority, and I met frequently with my counterparts at the two other libraries. Efforts included a conference for bibliographers at Michigan State University where progress was made toward identifying areas for cooperation. While I have not followed developments closely since I left the library, all three original collection development heads left for other positions as did the Deans/Directors of the three libraries. While the desire for cooperation remains strong, some of the earlier progress, based upon personal relationships, may have been lost.

In 1993, I left my position as Associate Dean to become a professor and then Director within the Wayne State University Library and Information Science Program. On occasion, I teach collection development where I have gained a larger perspective beyond academic libraries from readings for the course and from interacting with students who often have preprofessional experience in other types of libraries. Within the library, I continue to select materials in French language and literature because of my doctorate in French literature though I am no longer active in the administrative aspects of collection development.

My doctorate may also give me a different perspective from most other faculty members in library and information science. According to ALISE statistics, I am the only professor in our discipline with a doctorate in French though there are faculty with doctorates in other Humanities' subject areas. My disciplinary training has sensitized me to the need for monographs, full text, rare books, and manuscripts since literary studies depend less upon journal articles than many areas of the sciences and social sciences.

I wish to stress at this point that what follows is based upon my long experience in collection development and serious thinking about the issues. I also realize that I will often be making generalizations that could easily be contradicted in specific cases and that may reflect the factors that have influenced me. In addition, I have chosen to make this an opinion piece without references. My statements, however, are based upon my familiarity with the literature in the area of collection development. I believe that I could easily buttress my points of view with a critical apparatus if required to do so.

## THE PRE-INTERNET ERA

I believe that traditional cooperative collection development in the pre-Internet era was based upon the following assumptions.

### 1. Almost any item is potentially useful to some user.

My academic training predisposed me to the assumption, widely held by librarians, that almost any item in any format is of potential use to some user. Besides the fact that current research needs are hard to predict, future researchers may investigate new subjects and adopt new methodologies that will make items that currently appear of little value priceless. As a current example, diaries and journals of ordinary people, often preserved by accident since they did not reflect the deeds of the "great," have been mined by researchers who are now interested in how ordinary people lived. In fact, I have been a strong supporter of collecting popular culture materials in the belief that they will illuminate aspects of our culture that will be important for future researchers who wish to understand the complete spectrum of our experiences.

### 2. No one library can collect everything.

Even the largest libraries cannot collect everything theoretically worth keeping. Financial constraints may be the chief limiting factor with the high costs of acquiring, processing, storing, and preserving materials. Nonetheless, the shortage of expertise to identify, evaluate, and process materials is also a limiting factor since even mid-size to large research libraries cannot have experts in all subject disciplines of interest to even their primary clientele. I remember a meeting where the representatives from the Library of Congress (LC) were surprised to learn about the number of titles that they did not own but were held by other libraries in a subject area where LC's goal was to collect comprehensively.

## 3. Formal and informal diversification in collecting interests increases the number of unique items available to the user community.

Many research libraries of all types made the decision that it was justifiable to divert resources to create "spikes" of excellence rather than to raise or to maintain the general level of support to the current user community. Even with the end of growth in purchasing power for library materials and with the escalating costs of serials, many libraries nonetheless made the decision to reduce expenditures for "ordinary" materials, both monographs and serials, so that they could continue to purchase "esoteric" materials in areas of strength. Availability is one factor since the opportunity to purchase a rare book or materials from a Third World country is limited while standard published materials of the same value most often are available if user need requires them to be purchased in the future.

## 4. More libraries than might be assumed have a part to play in this interconnected informal system of making materials available for research.

I have purposely avoided using the term academic research library because I believe that many other types of libraries of all sizes have a role to play in making unique materials available for present and future research. While most academic research libraries build these "spikes" of excellence, so also do the large research public libraries. As a nearby example, the Detroit Public Library has taken on responsibility for collecting local history and also has an excellent automotive collection. Even smaller public libraries often collect local items that otherwise would be lost for research. Small targeted special libraries, whether in the profit or nonprofit sectors, do the same for limited subject areas though issues of access and availability may hinder widespread use.

## 5. Frequency of use and ease of access determine which materials are suitable for formal cooperative collection development.

Cooperative collection development assumes that libraries do not purchase certain materials but instead rely on other libraries to provide access to them. Materials in high demand by the library's primary clientele or that cannot be delivered quickly enough to the user are not suitable candidates for cooperative collection development. If, for whatever reason, a regularly offered undergraduate class depends upon "esoteric" materials for students to complete their assignments, the library will purchase these materials both because of their regular use and because of the need to make them available on a timely basis to a clientele that cannot wait.

Research and specialized materials are therefore the prime candidates for cooperative collection development for two main reasons: (a) most researchers do not require instant access and can wait to visit the holding library or to receive the documents through interlibrary loan; (b) the demands upon the holding library are not high enough to cause concern about diverting resources from the primary clientele. The cooperating libraries must agree to provide some form of equitable access to these materials to members of the cooperating group.

### 6. Formal cooperative collection development activities can take various forms.

In my experience, formal cooperative collection development activities fell into three categories:

- *Coordinating purchases of expensive items.* Cooperating libraries in a geographic area or consortium coordinate the purchase of expensive research materials. Generally, the library with the highest anticipated local use purchases the item.
- *Assigning primary subject collecting responsibility among the cooperating libraries.* These libraries decide to assign collection responsibility at a defined level to participating institutions. For example, one library might agree to purchase a high proportion of Australian fiction in English while others would do the same for Canada, Africa, and India.
- *Providing funds for a central agency to purchase materials.* The prime example of this strategy is the Center for Research Libraries (CRL) that pools member funds to purchase materials that otherwise would not be available to the North American research library community. In fact, one reason for non-purchase by CRL is the decision by member libraries to purchase the materials and make them available.

## 7. Traditional formal cooperative collection development is difficult to implement and, when implemented, is most often a time consuming and expensive activity.

Given the theoretical advantages of formal cooperative collection development, why has it been so difficult to implement and to maintain?

*A. Cooperation often requires a high degree of altruism in which participants do not closely monitor the costs and benefits since any agreement has winners and losers.* In fact, I believe that the most successful arrangements have included inducements or constraints from outside funding agencies to entice or to force libraries to participate. Examples include subsidies for interlibrary loan or major purchases or the allocation of funds that can only be spent cooperatively for the common good.

*B. Most of the time, not all partners will equally contribute to or benefit from the common pool.* While some research studies have shown that smaller institutions contribute more unique materials to the borrowing pool than is commonly thought, the worry persists that the larger institutions will contribute more and receive less. On the other hand, a smaller library with fewer resources may find it harder to meet its obligations from an outside agreement, especially when pressured by the multiple needs of its primary clientele.

*C. Cooperative collection development often raises access issues.* While cooperation most frequently involves research materials, formal agreements must often deal with reciprocal borrowing and onsite access for all types of users. It is difficult to limit access by undergraduate students or non-residents to the materials covered by the cooperative collection development agreement. Students with borrowing privileges, for example, may choose to use an academic library closer to their home if they commute or to make heavy use of another library during vacation, especially in states where major universities are located away from the population centers where students permanently reside.

*D. Cooperative collection development and resource sharing may encourage the inappropriate use of outside resources.* While I may be uttering library heresy, I believe that many academic assignments at the undergraduate and even graduate level can be successfully completed with the desired learning outcomes without using tempting outside resources. Let me explain. Especially for monographs, general subject headings often mask information on more specific topics that appear as subject headings in their own right for more specialized monographs. Students understandably want the specialized items that exactly match their topic and overlook the more general items that nonetheless contain useful and perhaps more appropriate information for the level of their assignments.

*E. Cooperative collection development requires adequate bibliographic control to make the items known to the users in the other libraries.* Owning an item is not enough. Users in the home institution and at the other participating libraries must be able to know that it exists in order to retrieve it. While bibliographic control has improved enormously, especially in the area of major microform sets, since my career began in the early 1970s, specialized research materials including manuscripts and archives often require expensive original cataloging. With outsourcing and the general reduction in the number of trained catalogers due to the phenomenal success of shared cataloging, expertise to catalog adequately these materials may be lacking. Even with adequate cataloging, printed or microform union lists and other finding tools for shared resources are cumbersome to use.

*F. Cooperative collection development is a dynamic process that requires continuous attention.* However detailed and effective an initial cooperative collection development agreement may be, the needs, interests, and capabilities of the participating libraries will change. Collection development in academic libraries should adjust to the educational objectives of the institution. Faculty leave; research interests shift; new programs arise; well-established programs disappear. Changes in collecting levels can then affect not only purchases for the primary clientele but also interest in participating in cooperative collection development. The change can be either wanting to abandon a subject area of reduced local interest or deciding to collect more heavily in an area given to another library with the resultant strain on the benefits from cooperation.

*G. Discrete subject areas may be difficult to identify.* The increased interdisciplinary nature of much research makes it difficult to identify discrete collecting areas for cooperative collection development. Since library classification schemes (LC and DDC) are based upon an outdated map of knowledge, new subject areas such as gerontology are not brought together.

*H. Cooperative collection development requires trust in the continuance of any agreements.* Library and university administrators also change. The willingness to participate in agreements and to provide reciprocal access can disappear. Even if a legal agreement exists, cooperation requires good will in addition to legal compliance. Especially for voluntary agreements without any outside funding or constraints, the trust element may make it difficult to enter into radical agreements where a library would have difficulty in meeting a portion of its mission if a partner pulled out.

*I. Cooperative collection development has overhead costs.* One major issue for cooperative collection has been how to reduce the overhead costs. In a profession that has a hard time distinguishing between costs and expenditures, direct expenditures in support of cooperative collection development may be low–funding for meetings and workshops, some additional paperwork, and membership in organizations like the Center for Research Libraries. Even the time that bibliographers spend in working out and implementing the agreements may be reasonable. The real costs are probably for additional document delivery where libraries encourage increased resource sharing as part of cooperative collection development. While I realize that libraries exist to provide such services, I return to Point D above about the costs of overlooking the primary collection to go elsewhere even when such use is not essential. I hope that others would agree with me that it is an inefficient use of resources for high school students to use the Library of Congress to write term papers. I also remember the director of a smaller library who described union catalogs as a candy store where his users would expect him to pay for the sweets through increased interlibrary loan.

## PRE-INTERNET CONCLUSIONS

While formal cooperative collection development is an appealing concept, I have concerns about its usefulness as I have described it above.

### *1. Administrators have misinterpreted the goal of cooperative collection development as a way to reduce collection expenditures.*

In my opinion, the achievable and desirable goal of cooperative collection development is expanding access to resources beyond those available to the participating library in a way that is more cost effective than purchasing the materials locally. I fear that many administrators have a different goal–to provide the same level of local access for less money than would otherwise be the case. To give a concrete example, membership in the Center for Research Libraries does not save local costs, except perhaps for the very largest academic libraries, but instead provides access to esoteric research materials in case of need. In fact, as I stated earlier, the decision by several libraries to purchase an item proposed by CRL is a reason for CRL to spend its available funds on something else. Furthermore, effective formal cooperative collection development agreements that assign primary collecting responsibilities by subject may require an increase in the acquisitions budget to provide comprehensive coverage in the agreed upon area. Finally, pressures on local collection development budgets have been such that items that could reasonably be predicted to have little or no use have already been eliminated in most research libraries. Attempting to cut local purchases more deeply in the name of cooperative collection development may be like paying for small losses with an insurance policy–much more costly in terms of money and service than it is worth.

## 2. Formal cooperative collection development agreements have unintended consequences.

As I suggested above, formal cooperative collection development agreements must deal with the issue of access and often do so in ways that encourage higher levels of cooperative collection use at no cost to the user. While I realize that books are for use and that the goal of a research library is to provide materials and services to its clientele, traditional delivery services such as interlibrary loan are expensive. Efforts to publicize the cooperative collection development agreement may have the unintended effect of encouraging users to think first of the largest collection in their subject area even if located at another library rather than making the most effective use of available local resources. They may also lead new classes of users, primarily undergraduate and masters' level students, to make heavier use of interlibrary loan. Improvements in the quality and speed of document delivery, while necessary for effective cooperative collection development, may also encourage higher use of the service for less than compelling reasons. Even economies of scale, though they may reduce the unit costs for each transaction, nonetheless increase the total expenditures to the library that, unlike a for-profit institution, does not directly receive increased revenue for increased and improved service delivery.

**3. In comparison with no agreements or informal agreements, formal cooperative collection development agreements may not be cost effective in reaching the goal of richer collective collection resources.**

My final point is that formal cooperative collection agreements may not have added that much value in increasing the number of unique resources available to researchers. The finding that collection overlap among libraries is less than could be expected indicates that the natural system of collection growth and specialization among libraries may work quite well. The differences in teaching and research interests among academic programs even in the same subject area and the varying interests of curators, bibliographers, and selectors may have led to greater collection diversity beyond the core collections that every research library must own to support its basic mission.

In fact, many formal agreements may only codify and make explicit what is already happening informally. A few telephone calls about major purchases do not require an elaborate agreement. The assignment of subject-based collecting areas most often follows institutional priorities that were already driving buying decisions. The contribution to a central collection facility is mandated by either outside bodies or a long-standing tradition.

To conclude this section, within the traditional pre-Internet constraints, going beyond what might have happened naturally and without formal agreements would be exceptionally resource intensive since the next level of decision making for cooperative collection development would have required evaluating materials on an item-by-item basis, a difficult process in pre-Internet days.

## THE INTERNET ERA

I believe that the Internet and the World Wide Web (WWW) have already begun to change profoundly cooperative collection development and will have future consequences that are dangerous to predict. I will begin with the positive changes.

**1. The Internet provides interconnectivity that resolves many barriers to effective cooperative collection development.**

*A. Bibliographers can more easily check holdings at other institutions.* One barrier to item-by-item cooperative collection development was the difficulty in checking holdings at other institutions. I realize that the bibliographic utilities (OCLC, RLIN, and WLN) have provided holdings information for many years; but access required expensive, dedicated terminals that were either not available to bibliographers, required making special efforts to find an available terminal, or caused delays as support staff did the bibliographic checking. With the Internet, access to the bibliographic utilities is available on the desktop computer. Online catalogs and other finding tools are readily available on the World Wide Web or through direct connections. Computer multitasking allows the bibliographer to move seamlessly among the sources that need to be checked. Standards such as Z39.50 make it possible to repeat the search in multiple systems with minimal rekeying. Cooperative collection development on an item-by-item basis has suddenly become feasible.

*B. E-mail and file transfer simplify communication among bibliographers.* I continue to be amazed at how important email has become in simplifying communication, especially where detailed information is concerned. Beyond a simple consultation on a few items, it is possible to transfer large machine-readable files that have already been created for other purposes and that are computer searchable and manipulatable by the recipient.

*C. Users have direct access to bibliographic and full-text data.* Users most often have the same direct access as bibliographers and can query outside resources for bibliographic information either through gateways on their local systems or through the Internet, principally the World Wide Web. Depending upon the system, they can have access by author, title, keyword, subject, and classification. As will be discussed below, they may be able to retrieve the full text for the items that they want. Thus, they can make more effective use of any cooperative collection development agreements by locating appropriate resources on their own.

*D. Users can take responsibility for many tasks associated with document delivery.* Given the significant overhead for document delivery in pre-Internet days, perhaps one of the most important positive developments is that users can now order documents directly without library staff intervention. When full text is available, the user can complete the entire transaction on the desktop and download the document directly to the computer or printer. As I stated above, these new capabilities bring up the potential negative of increased volume leading to higher library expenditures for the service. But the increase in service benefits to the user and the reduction of associated costs that are not service enhancements (ILL staffing, paper handling, record keeping, etc.) should make these changes exceptionally cost effective.

**2. Digitization is a key element in cooperative collection development.**

Once resources are available digitally, the issue of multiple locations and availability practically disappears. The distribution of computer software through ftp sites could be a model since the Internet effectively eliminates the issue of distance and replication. Users could locate desired materials through either traditional library catalogs or sophisticated search engines that would perhaps be limited to library materials and download the documents to their desktops. The question will be whether these reservoirs of digital resources exist in libraries or elsewhere. In the second case, libraries will have a much less prominent place in the scholarly communication system.

Many obstacles hinder realization of this objective, including the cost of digitization, copyright, and the necessity of recouping costs in an environment where it would be extremely difficult to control the reuse of electronic texts. An even more fundamental question is how to retain the financial incentives for the creation of new knowledge.

I also have some concerns about cooperative collection development in the Internet era.

**1. Electronic resources and their required infrastructure will compete for funds with traditional library resources whose purchasing power has already been reduced by the high inflation in serial prices.**

Research libraries will need to make major new funding decisions. The new electronic resources are not cheap and are often purchased with monies that otherwise would have been spent on traditional library materials. Cooperative collection development today may mean programs to share the cost of expensive commercial electronic resources rather than building the research storehouse of unique items. Squeezed by funding for electronic resources and serials inflation, research libraries are tempted to reduce purchases of non-mainstream monographs and low use serials, often the most important components for cooperative collection development.

## 2. Library administrators and librarians will pay less attention to collection development.

It is my perception that library administrators and the new generation of librarians are paying less attention to collection development in general. The tradition of the scholar librarian with extensive knowledge of the collection may be waning. It is difficult to become knowledgeable about a virtual collection. While I will not argue against the validity of the concept of "access rather than ownership" or of "just in time rather than just in case," this change diminishes the importance of the tradition of bibliographers and curators who strive to build the best possible collections to meet specific institutional needs. Finally, the library profession through its culture, education, and reward system currently favors information technology over the older and more mundane tradition of building quality collections.

## 3. Library collections are becoming more homogenous, and this factor works against cooperative collection development.

With research libraries under pressure to provide more service with less funding, collection development seems to be following the path taken by cataloging over the last thirty years. Individual libraries are increasingly depending upon outside agencies to provide materials to reduce the personnel costs related to collection development. While approval plans, blanket orders, and outsourcing may make the most effective use of resources, these efficiencies may come at the price of increased homogeneity of collections. Spikes of excellence and diversity of holdings may require more of a conscious decision than in the past.

**4. The Internet may lead to a devaluing of traditional library materials.**

The emphasis upon the Internet and the richness of resources on the World Wide Web may cause librarians and researchers to devalue traditional library resources and pay much less attention to them. In addition, resources that might have appeared in print format may migrate to the WWW. Materials that are accessible, at least for the moment to everyone with a Web browser, are certainly not candidates for cooperative collection development.

**5. The Internet may kill once and for all the myth that it is possible to collect and store all potentially useful information.**

The WWW contains so much information that varies extremely in quality and is subject to such constant change that the long held myth of collecting and storing all potentially useful human information (knowledge) can no longer be maintained. While it may be possible to capture some of this storehouse of information, the sheer volume makes it impossible to retain a complete permanent record in any useable format. The death of the myth may also cause libraries to reexamine the same myth as it affects traditional materials and to decide to concentrate more on relevance and useability than on comprehensiveness.

## THE FUTURE

I believe that the age of judging research libraries by the size of their collections has passed. Access as the new paradigm holds great appeal in comparison with the costs of acquiring, processing, housing, and preserving traditional "just in case" research collections. What then will be the future for cooperative collection development?

**1. Research libraries will focus their collection development efforts more on materials of immediate use to their primary clientele.**

With no end in sight to the funding pressures enumerated above, research libraries will focus on materials with a high probability of use including expensive electronic resources. The willingness and the ability to fund "spikes" of excellence will diminish and, with them, the ability to participate in formal and informal cooperative collection development. The largest research libraries will still continue to collect intensively in their areas of excellence and could possibly receive outside support to do so from government and private funding agencies and from fees for interlibrary loan.

**2. Some specialized research materials will migrate to the WWW and ease the pressure for cooperative collection development of print formats.**

Cooperative collection development has often focused on materials that are not necessarily expensive but that are difficult to acquire and to process. These materials including ephemera, grey literature, small press publications, polemical tracts, etc., may migrate to the WWW. This migration will bring about other collection development issues that are beyond the scope of this paper.

**3. Cooperative collection development in the future may mean providing financial support to the libraries with the best subject collections to continue to collect intensively and to digitize existing and future collections.**

The advantages of access to extensive digital collections are so great that the research community may find ways to overcome the significant obstacles to this goal. Reaching this goal may depend upon finding ways to enhance and to extend current efforts in cooperative preservation. I believe that research libraries would be willing to fund the Center for Research Libraries at higher levels if their users had access to a large storehouse of digitized information that could be accessed directly from their desktops.

**4. Many researchers may concentrate on available digitized resources and not worry about print materials.**

While I am less sure of this prediction, as the decades pass, many researchers may decide that the WWW and other digital resources provide enough material that they can overlook printed resources.

Only very serious scholars will mine print information, which will become to future scholars what archival materials were to the scholars of the print age. This new attitude will reduce the impetus that led to cooperative collection development in the first place.

## *CONCLUSION*

I will conclude by saying that I am often asked about the future of libraries and librarianship. I respond that great changes lie ahead but that it is much too early to make accurate predictions. Who foresaw the importance of the WWW a decade ago? The impetus among librarians to collect and to preserve the largest amount of human knowledge possible will endure, though the practical mutations to reach this goal cannot be foreseen. While I mourn the passing of the myth of preserving all human knowledge and the role of cooperative collection development in reaching this goal, I remain excited about what lies ahead.

# The Center for Research Libraries and Cooperative Collection Development: Partnerships in Progress

Gay N. Dannelly

**SUMMARY.** The environment for cooperative collection efforts has significantly altered in the last five years due to online public access catalogs, technology changes, and economic realities. One of the most effective mechanisms for establishing a cooperative collection agenda including providing access to a much richer bank of resources, making the most economical use of funds, and setting a shared political agenda is the establishment of library consortia. The changes that have made this a viable model are considered in light of the role of the Center for Research Libraries (CRL) as a partner in the cooperative collection development agenda. *[Article copies available for a fee from The Haworth Document Delivery Service: 1-800-342-9678. E-mail address: getinfo@haworthpressinc.com]*

Cooperative collection development has a long history but that history is, for the most part, fragmented consisting of short-term agreements or programs such as the Farmington Plan; or narrowly focused initiatives such as the banding together of small, local colleges to maximize savings and access. The Research Libraries Group has had the most ambitious program, but even their efforts have shifted from cooperative collection development efforts to a different set of initiatives and programs. These have all been worthy efforts that have attempted to fulfill specific needs at specific times. But the political

---

Gay N. Dannelly is Assistant Director for Collections and Associate Professor at the Ohio State University Libraries.

[Haworth co-indexing entry note]: "The Center for Research Libraries and Cooperative Collection Development: Partnerships in Progress." Dannelly, Gay N. Co-published simultaneously in *Collection Management* (The Haworth Press, Inc.) Vol. 23, No. 4, 1998, pp. 37-45; and: *Cooperative Collection Development: Significant Trends and Issues* (ed: Donald B. Simpson) The Haworth Press, Inc., 1998, pp. 37-45. Single or multiple copies of this article are available for a fee from The Haworth Document Delivery Service [1-800-342-9678, 9:00 a.m. - 5:00 p.m. (EST). E-mail address: getinfo@haworthpressinc.com].

infrastructure and functional capabilities that are necessary for continuity of effort, reliability of information provision, and mechanisms for the efficient and effective delivery of resources did not yet exist in forms that worked sufficiently well to be acceptable to the majority of institutions.

## COOPERATIVE COLLECTION DEVELOPMENT ISSUES

During the December 1997 online discussion of cooperative collection development issues hosted by the Center for Research Libraries and published elsewhere in this issue, a variety of concerns facing collection development in general and cooperative efforts specifically, were identified and considered by the participants. Specific themes that recurred with great regularity were: trust between institutions, utility of materials, reliability of partner institutions, mechanisms for delivery and logistics of delivery, speed of delivery of required information, differentiation of needs among fields of study, costs, and political imperatives. Each of these elements plays a part in the development of dependable, accepted cooperative relationships.

Cooperative collection development has traditionally been viewed as a matter of selection, requiring two or more bibliographers and libraries to agree to parse their collections in specific ways. However, as Susan Rabe noted in the CRL discussion, ". . . local needs will continue to determine selection. If this is the case, then cooperative collection development is not about selection but about cooperating to build a collective collection by sharing information about what is in each collection (bibliographic access, union lists of serial holdings, copy information, etc.) and sharing physical access to those collections."

## THE ENVIRONMENT FOR COOPERATIVE COLLECTION DEVELOPMENT

The environment for cooperative collection efforts has significantly altered in the last five years due to online public access catalogs, the Internet, and economic realities. And it has become clear that one of the most effective mechanisms for establishing a cooperative collection agenda including providing access to a much richer bank of resources, making the most economical use of funds, and setting a shared political agenda is the establishment of library consortia. In fact, not even the largest and best-supported libraries can afford not to join a consortium. University Presidents and Provosts love them (and unfortunately often see such membership as a way to decrease commitments to the local library); faculty feel threatened by them until they see the resources that become available to them and to their students; and students want them to work faster!

In order for such programs to be effective, however, there needs to be an adequate delivery mechanism; an area that has in the past been the primary reason for the failure of cooperative programs. The advent of shared on-line public access catalogs, electronic document delivery and the use of object delivery mechanisms, such as Federal Express and other carriers, has become the lifeblood of consortia. Even the economic incentives of shared funding and reduced costs cannot outweigh the importance of effective document delivery.

In this new environment, many issues come to the surface and influence the way cooperative collection development can work. The first, and perhaps most difficult barrier to cooperation is the tension between local priorities and group priorities. Participation in a consortium can (and should) change the way local resources are selected, thus changing the culture of collection development at the local level and changing the way collection managers/selectors work with their subject faculty and graduate students. In many ways, this is the most difficult issue to be faced by the cooperative venture. It is very hard to change the practices of the past, and the feeling of every bibliographer that his or her role is to build the best, most complete, collection possible in a specific discipline or area of study. It is at least as difficult to change faculty perceptions and expectations, particularly when the library community still measures library effectiveness and rank only by local holdings. However, the real value in consortial cooperatives, aside from economic and political incentives, is the opportunity to build a shared information base from which to provide expanded resources and services at the local level.

## *THE IMPACT OF ON-LINE ACCESS*

The on-line catalog and access via the Internet have changed the expectation of faculty, graduate students and undergraduates as well.

The ease with which any individual can identify the existence and location of a specific item is remarkable. Of course, the item's availability to the remote user is not necessarily obvious to the requestor, but the ease of finding the item does set up expectations that Interlibrary Loan can often be hard pressed to meet. The potential for meeting such expectations, however, is vastly increased by the ability to establish a centralized catalog within a consortia or by the application of Z39.50 search mechanisms that can search across several catalogs at one time using local search strategies. The combination of these searching mechanisms with patron initiated requesting (available in OhioLINK and the CIC [Committee for Institutional Cooperation] Virtual Catalog), and an effective delivery mechanism provides the structure that is necessary to make cooperative collection development a viable and effective program amongst a variety of university, college and technical school libraries.

Both the Illinois and OhioLINK cooperative systems experiences demonstrate that it is not the large institutions that, necessarily, provide the majority of loaned materials. Rather the large institutions become the greatest borrowers since they can then access items that their libraries own but that are in circulation. Clearly the larger collections provide the greatest diversity of resources, but this is only one element of the content of a cooperative collection development arrangement.

## BUDGETARY IMPLICATIONS OF COOPERATIVE COLLECTION DEVELOPMENT

In general, the first initiative for cooperative collection development and resource sharing programs is to save money and to improve access to a wider array of information resources. In some cases, such as that of the CIC or the University of California system, there are institutional imperatives that both initiate and mandate cooperation across a variety of programs, the library being only one area of concern. In other situations, funding at the state level can be the imperative and can operate outside of institutional funding or priorities, essentially changing the institutional environment by mandating broader cooperative efforts among the libraries in the state. This is clearly the case with OhioLINK, a program composed of a shared central catalog, individual institutional catalogs, shared databases and a wide variety of full-text resources, primarily funded by the Ohio Board of Regents as a separate line item in the budget and operating as a separate entity.

Budget support for libraries has shown a continuing pattern of erosion for many years. Association of Research Libraries statistical reports reflect a regular decline in the Education and General Budget Expenditures for library support across all institutions. In some cases this is mitigated by large endowments, but in general the percentage of the institutional budget expended in support of library materials and services is decreasing as the costs of library materials increase at a rate that is significantly higher than the Consumer Price Index.

## THE ELECTRONIC INFORMATION EXPLOSION

Into an environment of decreasing budgetary support for library programs, the electronic information explosion brings another set of programmatic imperatives that include increased costs both for access and for the infrastructure necessary to support their use. There is a direct competition between the needs for electronic information resources, both indices and full-text, and the needs of the traditional collections. The differential shifts from paper to digital format by discipline and by area of study serve only to complicate further an already difficult area of change.

Licensing of digital resources requires an ever-increasing investment of staff time in the library as well as in the institutional contracts or legal office. The provisions of differing contracts require a variety of systems management and access mechanisms and a constant monitoring of contract renewals and their changing requirements over time. The ways in which publishers and vendors provide digital content differ and each requires a set of negotiations that make the contract process almost as expensive as the content itself (or at least it feels that way on some days).

## THE CHANGING NATURE OF COLLECTION DEVELOPMENT

As the downsizing trends in staffing continue in higher education and are manifested in the library, we see less and less attention available for collection development of local collections and thereby less attention to those elements that may fuel cooperative programs. The approval plan programs that have been put in place to simply acquire materials without review may make sense institutionally, but they also send a signal to the external world that collections are less important and that attention is paid to short term goals and short term applications of efficiency rather than the careful crafting of collections. The reasons given for such programs is often to free the time of selectors to give more attention to selection outside the mainstream, but the real result seems to be to turn the attention of already scarce personnel to other areas and to skimp even further on collection development.

The changing nature of higher education and the funding of libraries brings the issue of cooperative collection development to a head in the priorities of many institutions. Local cooperative initiatives take priority and other longstanding agreements may fall by the wayside. However, as the local projects develop it is important not only to integrate those resources held by the immediate members, but to seek ways to integrate across consortial lines and one of the most strategic collections to include in any cooperative effort is that of the Center for Research Libraries.

## THE CENTER FOR RESEARCH LIBRARIES: AN AGENT FOR COOPERATIVE COLLECTION DEVELOPMENT

The Center for Research Libraries (CRL) has developed a set of program initiatives that embody many of the elements of cooperative collection development identified earlier in this paper (trust, reliability, etc.). It has clear directions for the collection of print resources that are recognized by its membership and by the scholarly community in general. The clarity of its vision and its effective implementation have given CRL a standard to meet as the academy moves into the future of digital information and the as-yet-unsolved issues of archiving of that information.

Some institutions view the Center solely as a cost item that can potentially be recovered and directed elsewhere. However, the experience that Ohio State and OhioLINK have had with CRL has shown that the costs are well worth the investment and that the needs of faculty and graduate students in particular are well served by the

Center's collections. As our local funds are siphoned off to pay for scientific, technical and medical journals, the Center continues to provide considerable value for the funds invested by supporting our humanities and social sciences with both expensive and little used, but strategic, collections of national importance. We have also found that the consortial membership of OhioLINK in the Center for Research Libraries is already paying dividends to the many Ohio faculty and graduate students, including those at many small institutions that would never have considered membership in CRL, but whose faculty are better able to further their research programs with the support of materials not only from OhioLINK, but also from the Center.

Ohio State has had CRL bibliographic records in the on-line catalog for several years, but with the patron initiated request capacity added through the OhioLINK system, our filled requests increased by 10% during the period of July 1, 1995-June 30, 1996 (the latest period for which statistics are available). During the same period, University of Akron, University of Dayton, and Case Western Reserve filled requests decreased, while six other institutions increased their use, in two cases by 414% and 118% (which sounds incredible) and smaller institutions borrowed 629 items that they would not have been able to access prior to the consortial membership. It remains to be seen if the patterns of use will change significantly or if those institutions that decreased use will change and increase their use. The overall change in use in OhioLINK, however, is a total increase in use of 67%, with some institutions clearly making significant increases in use.

Admittedly, the OhioLINK model is thus far an unusual one. However, a variety of other library groups are negotiating to develop similar programmatic structures to enhance their use of CRL through consortial arrangements. It is an evolutionary process that should increase not only the membership profile of CRL but also the use of its collections and recognition of the importance of these collections to the scholarly community.

## CRL AND FUTURE COOPERATIVE COLLECTION DEVELOPMENT INITIATIVES

In the world of cyberspace, libraries have a variety of collection imperatives that will require thoughtful consideration, a bit of crystal ball gazing and a concomitant recognition of economic realities. To develop a significant role in this future, the Center needs to carefully craft a set of future initiatives that enhance its role in the scholarly community and that retain the centrality of its collections and its mission as libraries move into the digital environment. Such initiatives should build on the strength of CRL's present collections to establish cooperative imperatives such as those already in place for South Asia and Akademie Nauk collections. In both cases CRL joined and to a great extent led the national efforts for coordinated collections in these areas.

The Center needs to seek ways in which to apply technology to make better use of collections, such as the partnerships with Ohio-LINK and other consortia. This is particularly strategic to improving the visibility of CRL in smaller institutions.

The Center needs to evaluate its role as the scholarly electronic collection of little-used materials, analogous to its present role in the paper world. The digital world is not yet as coherent as the paper world (which in itself is damning with faint praise), but CRL must chart a future that includes digital collections and programs if it is to maintain its centrality to the scholarly community and serve as the collection of last resort in the future. These initiatives need to address the commercial market as well as the "free" market of the Internet as CRL is beginning to do with the former CIC Electronic Journal Collection.

It is important for the Center to craft these new initiatives so that it continues to support its traditional mission in ways that take advantage of the new technologies, but also maintains and enhances the scholarly nature of the collections.

## *CONCLUSION*

At present, the Center acquires specific materials and has very clear collection priorities and programs. The CRL membership needs to expand these into the digital world as they become appropriate and seek to develop a collection for the future that takes advantage of both the scholarly nature of the present collections and the access and delivery mechanisms of the future. The archiving of digital materials is probably the single most difficult and complex issue facing the scholarly information community at present. CRL must be a partner in that enterprise both for its corporate future and as a trusted and reliable player in the provision of historical collections in North America and the rest of the scholarly world.

The fiftieth anniversary of the Center is an appropriate time to celebrate its long-term role as one of the oldest effective cooperative collection development tools in the research library arsenal of programs. It is also a time to set a new agenda to carry the Center into the future and to chart a program that perpetuates its centrality to the scholarly community of information resources.

# The Role of the Center for Research Libraries in the History and Future of Cooperative Collection Development

Linda A. Naru

**SUMMARY.** Almost fifty years ago, when the organization that now is the Center for Research Libraries (CRL) was founded, university and research libraries were facing issues similar to those challenging them today: lack of space in libraries to shelve growing collections; new library materials formats to absorb into acquisitions budgets; more or more expensive research materials to which patrons needed access.

In 1949, higher education looked for solutions in cooperative programs. CRL evolved as a unique endeavor–a program for cooperative collection development and a library that acquires and makes available essential research materials. CRL has endured because of its members' commitment, the gradual building of a unique, centralized library collection, and the organization's capacity to serve as a coordinator for cooperative decisions and implementation of programs. These strengths will support CRL into the future. *[Article copies available for a fee from The Haworth Document Delivery Service: 1-800-342-9678. E-mail address: getinfo@haworthpressinc.com]*

## INTRODUCTION

The building which we dedicate today houses a co-operative effort that ... produces economies, that is true; but its justifica-

---

Linda A. Naru is Director of Member Services at the Center for Research Libraries, Chicago, IL.

[Haworth co-indexing entry note]: "The Role of the Center for Research Libraries in the History and Future of Cooperative Collection Development." Naru, Linda A. Co-published simultaneously in *Collection Management* (The Haworth Press, Inc.) Vol. 23, No. 4, 1998, pp. 47-58; and: *Cooperative Collection Development: Significant Trends and Issues* (ed: Donald B. Simpson) The Haworth Press, Inc., 1998, pp. 47-58. Single or multiple copies of this article are available for a fee from The Haworth Document Delivery Service [1-800-342-9678, 9:00 a.m. - 5:00 p.m. (EST). E-mail address: getinfo@haworthpressinc.com].

© 1998 by The Haworth Press, Inc. All rights reserved.

tion rests primarily in the fact that *it increases the educational resources that are available to the member institutions.*

*—Ernest C. Colwell[1]*

The words that resonate through the fifty years of the history of the Center for Research Libraries (CRL) are that cooperative collection development increases the education resources available to researchers, students, and faculty at member institutions. CRL's guiding precept since its establishment as the Midwest Inter-Library Center in 1949, is that a cooperative approach to collecting and making accessible specific kinds of library research materials will leverage resources and expand the universe of materials available to North American scholars.

To do collection development and management, librarians use a toolbox of subject specialization, written policies, professional acumen, political savvy, budget sensitivity, and a collegial network of information and support. Providing the most resources possible within the constraints of physical or budgetary reality is a primary goal of collection development. One means to reach this goal is through formal cooperative agreements with other libraries to share library collections. For almost fifty years, CRL has provided a framework for coordinated decision-making and a physical place in which to implement these decisions.

As CRL approaches its fiftieth anniversary in 1999, research librarians are concerned with local priorities in collection development that include the following:

- managing budgetary constraints that necessitate strategic journals cancellations and other acquisition curtailments
- sharing library materials budgets with new media, especially electronic publications, or new costs, such as licensing fees
- preserving print and electronic materials
- serving remote users
- serving users who have increasing demands resulting from their sophistication in accessing research tools

How are these issues facing research libraries at the end of the 1990s related to the questions that led to the establishment of CRL?

What role will CRL play during the next fifty years to "increase the educational resources available to [its] member institutions"?

## WHY WAS CRL ESTABLISHED?

The origins of a depository library in the midwestern part of the U.S.–what eventually became CRL–began in the 1930s. In 1940, thirteen university presidents from the region formally investigated the design, costs, collections and administration of a cooperative deposit library. The Carnegie Corporation financed a survey to study the possibility of establishing a cooperative storage and distribution center for little-used books from the collections of the thirteen university libraries: the University of Chicago, the University of Illinois, Indiana University, Iowa State College, the State University of Iowa, the University of Kentucky, Michigan State College, the University of Michigan, the University of Minnesota, Northwestern University, Ohio State University, Purdue University, and the University of Wisconsin. John Fall, from the New York Public Library, coordinated the survey under the supervision of Keyes D. Metcalf of Harvard University. The results of the survey were summarized in a report entitled "A Proposal for a Middle West Deposit Library."[2]

Fall's report contains many points about the objectives of economical storage, preservation and increased availability of infrequently used materials. The 1940 proposal concentrated on the arguments for establishing a storage facility, but included the idea that the deposit library eventually would have cooperative purchase and preservation programs. The primary economic benefits of cooperative storage were that institutions could defer construction of library buildings and, consequently, be able to accumulate cash reserves and use the savings to develop other library services; in addition, removing little-used materials from library stacks would eliminate recurring expenses to maintain and shift these volumes.

The preservation benefits of a cooperative storage facility were that a new building would be fireproof and offer protection against excessive heat, light, dust, and other harmful elements.

The proposal covered specific planning points including the following: geographic location and the factors of proximity to transportation, to a large "book population," and to microfilming facilities; whether to assess a flat fee or to base fees on the amount of use; whether or not to limit the kinds of libraries that could participate or to include governmental and public libraries; staffing, particularly the sufficiency of a 1.5 full-time equivalent staff, and the classes of books that would be accepted as deposits, including newspapers, old periodicals, textbooks, books in seldom-used foreign languages, superseded publications, and outdated materials in applied science and technology.

Although the thirteen university presidents were in agreement that the deposit library would solve their pressing local space problems, the university librarians were cautious about the impact of a cooperative collection on their own libraries. The deposit library discussion was deferred until 1947.

When the university presidents raised the question of a depository library again in 1947, the library directors formulated a plan with four programmatic aspects: coordination of collection policies, centralized cataloging, cooperative storage of little-used materials, and cooperative acquisitions. The cooperative acquisitions program began when MILC opened for business in 1951, with the entering of subscriptions to forty newspapers in microfilm. However, the functions of centralized cataloging and coordination of collection policies proved unworkable.

The articles of incorporation define CRL's purposes:

> To establish and maintain an educational, literary, scientific, charitable and research interlibrary center; to provide and promote co-operative, auxiliary services for one or more non-profit educational, charitable and scientific institutions; to establish, conduct and maintain a place or places for the deposit, storage, care, delivery and exchange of books . . . and other articles containing written, printed, or recorded matter, and services with respect thereto.[3]

## WHAT ARE CRL'S CONTRIBUTIONS TO COOPERATIVE COLLECTION DEVELOPMENT?

In 1949, when CRL began, academic libraries looked to this organization to solve these problems: how to acquire increasing numbers of materials printed outside of the U.S.; how to create more shelving space in library buildings filled to capacity; how to meet researchers' demands for access to materials in languages other than English; how to store and make available to users the relatively new media of microformats.

For the past fifty years, CRL members have contributed time, expertise, involvement, and funding to meet these problems. The accomplishments of the members' cooperative collection development program include these:

- *A large and strong research library collection.* CRL members built a library collection of more than 5 million items that supports research in virtually all humanities, social sciences, and pure and applied sciences. Seventy percent of CRL's holdings were published outside of the U.S., and 62% of cataloged titles are in languages other than English.
- *Comprehensive coverage of types of materials.* CRL is the definitive source for specialized holdings that are comprehensive in subject, geographic coverage, and date of printing and, as an integral collection, are the premier source for such materials: for example, the foreign dissertation collection is a dynamic and comprehensive collection of doctoral dissertations written at universities outside of the U.S. and Canada.
- *A high-density book storage facility.* During the 1950s, CRL members deposited almost 2 million printed volumes and microforms weeded from their local library collections but deemed to have research value for the library community as a whole. The deposit function continues to be available (under the collection development policy guidelines) to relieve libraries of shelving space problems.
- *Continuing commitments to rarely-held serials, newspapers, etc.* Current acquisitions programs focus on research materials that are not collected in other libraries: serials with fewer than 20 North American library holdings; foreign and domestic newspapers; foreign dissertations; archival materials recording the activities of national governments, etc.
- *A means to facilitate expert national collaboration among research libraries.* CRL's policy development structure utilizes the talents of librarians, subject specialists, and faculty who serve on the CRL committees and working groups to formulate and review collection development policies. CRL's collection policy also is a guideline for local library collecting, and major universi-

ties and research institutions in the U.S. and Canada have shaped their libraries' collections based on CRL's holdings.
- *Leveraged dollars for acquisitions and processing.* Purchasing and processing costs (acquisitions, cataloging, shelving, etc.) for materials added to a decentralized library collection are distributed among all member libraries, resulting in very low costs. For example, in 1996/97, each of the 162 member libraries paid an average of seven cents per volume (in acquisitions costs) to add more than 108,000 volumes to the collection.

## WHAT ARE THE CHARACTERISTICS OF COOPERATIVE COLLECTION DEVELOPMENT IN CRL'S MODEL?

Cooperative enterprises enable libraries to provide more resources and thereby expand researchers' access to materials. These benefits are balanced by the requirements of each member library's commitment, involvement, and dedication to the cooperative collection building effort.

Certain characteristics define CRL's cooperative collection development endeavor:

- An institution (usually a university) is the membership unit, not the library. This provision places the goals of CRL into the broader context of the goals of higher education.
- Revenue to support CRL's library acquisitions, storage, and access is derived primarily from member dues.
- There is common (corporate) ownership of the library materials.
- The library materials are housed in a central library storage facility, not distributed among cooperating libraries.
- Collection access for a library and its users is assured only with continuing CRL membership: unlimited access to the collection is only for current members, and an institution can change its membership status annually.
- The majority rules in membership issues of governance and policy making.
- Membership fees support all collection programs, and each member participates in all collection programs; i.e., there is no unbundling of fees or services.
- The collection development policy is organized by area of the world or by publication format and by types of publications such

as dissertations, newspapers, etc. This necessitates an interdisciplinary approach to the collection, rather than subject selection used in most research libraries.

## HOW DOES CRL WORK TODAY?

Current CRL functions are dedicated to maintaining and building the cooperatively developed collections; incorporating new media into acquisitions, preservation and delivery processes; and improving bibliographic and physical access to its resources.

The collection development policy and collection descriptions are being simplified so that members can easily incorporate them into local policies. CRL's online catalog is accessible through the Internet, and users throughout the world can access the collection development policy (as well as other collection guides and descriptions) on CRL's Website.

Through the Brazilian Government Documents Digitization Project, CRL is developing expertise in digitizing, storing and making available materials in electronic format. In 1998, CRL will assume management of an electronic journals project begun by the libraries of the Committee on Institutional Cooperation. This initiative will expand CRL's experience in cataloging, archiving, and maintaining publisher relations for materials in electronic format.

CRL's staff resources and recent grant funds have been concentrated on cataloging unique materials, particularly monographs published by the Russian Academy of Sciences and foreign newspapers. A high priority is resolving the problem of providing bibliographic access to foreign dissertations, a growing collection component that now includes more than 750,000 titles and that has not been cataloged in accordance with a policy decision made at CRL's founding.

Users of library resources are becoming more independent of librarians, even in the resource sharing arena. In 1997, CRL began to fill requests initiated by patrons for loan of monographs. CRL's involvement to date has been part of a carefully planned program of OhioLINK, a cooperative venture of Ohio university libraries and the Ohio Board of Regents; however, CRL service directly to all patrons–including delivery of loaned materials and copies–is in the formative stages.

## WHAT IS CRL'S FUTURE IN COOPERATIVE COLLECTION DEVELOPMENT?

Having survived the struggle for establishment in the 1930s and 1940s, and nearing its fiftieth anniversary with many of its reasons for founding still of absorbing concern to research libraries and higher education, CRL is an organization looking toward the future. The spirit of the organization, unique collections, and some practical advantages will be important factors in the fifty-first year and onward.

### *A Large, Strong, and Unique Research Library Collection*

The unique CRL collection that has resulted from fifty years of the members' cooperative collection development decisions is not reproducible. In the 1950s, libraries deaccessioned and sent to CRL certain materials with unanticipated value that we are realizing today: many titles deposited in the early decades now are sources for contemporary research interests; for example, serials issued in the late nineteenth and early twentieth century on science and technology now support work in the history of science, and works of popular fiction or monographs on domestic arts now are focuses of women's studies. Early decisions to collectively select major reprint and microform sets and to subscribe to newspapers in microform gave CRL the foundation for building substantial retrospective collections of monographs, serials, and newspapers.

Member libraries have built CRL's collection as an integral subset of their local libraries, and CRL's is a collection to which they need continuing access. Even as more of the contents of great libraries become accessible in electronic files, most of the retrospective holdings of research libraries will remain in the paper or microform medium; CRL must continue to house and preserve indefinitely its exceptional collections.

### *The Historical Partnership of CRL with and Among Its Members*

One of CRL's defining characteristics that will continue to be a source of strength is its cooperative nature. As a union of university, college and research libraries, CRL has a broad base of support in higher education and the ability to impact thousands of researchers, faculty and students with each of its actions to make information more accessible. Many CRL members are skillful participants in cooperative endeavors and work easily in a framework of cooperation. For example, many of the CRL founding and current universities are members of the Committee on Institutional Cooperation (CIC), a group that advances the goals of its fourteen participants in technology, academics, athletics, etc.

Technology will help research library partnerships improve cooperative acquisitions decisions and make better use of resources. As it becomes easier to analyze collections by sorting through data elements in computerized catalogs and by consulting online catalogs available through the Internet, cooperative decisions will be more informed by current and accurate information on holdings, current journal receipts, preservation status. The founders' goal to coordinate collection policies will draw closer to realization.

## CRL Has Library Holdings That Meet Diverse Audiences' Needs for Certain Types of Materials for Research

It is an odd circumstance of library research that patrons' needs for resources sometimes transcend subject disciplines and simply require specific kinds of materials. CRL's library holdings are rich in materials collected originally by format–especially newspapers, foreign dissertations, foreign documents, and pre-1950 monographs and serials deposited by members–but now fulfill research needs in various subjects.

The best example from CRL's holdings of a material format that has broad appeal is the international collection of newspapers, built upon the goals of the Association of Research Libraries' newspaper project to preserve and to assure continuing access to one of the most ephemeral kinds of publications. Researchers' uses of a newspaper file from the 1860s run the gamut from contemporary reviews of Verdi opera performances to foreign perspectives on the American Civil War to consumer goods prices to legal cases to demographic information to changing weather conditions to subjects of religious sermons to mortality causes. Few academic libraries could maintain a collection of more than 6,500 foreign newspaper titles and thousands of United States papers for occasional research consultation; however, CRL's patron audience is the total of 162 universities', colleges', and research libraries' clientele from various academic disciplines who in the aggregate make frequent use of these collections.

## Research Libraries Face More Demands on Their Budgets, Diverting More Resources from the Acquisition of Lower-Demand Materials

Recent trends indicate the increasing diversion of acquisitions funds to leasing electronic resources; this is a further erosion of "book money" that libraries endure along with continuing waves of escalating journals costs.

Libraries prevented from maintaining comprehensive collections locally can continue to supplement their research-level collections by accessing the most esoteric levels of materials from CRL. CRL always has held items consulted by the most serious scholars and very little of the basic library materials. Segmenting acquisitions responsibility–libraries buying high-demand items and CRL buying less frequently used materials–is an efficient strategy to insure the broadest coverage of available research library materials.

## CRL's Building Capacity and Shelving Space

CRL's physical plant is new (constructed in 1982 and 1993) and environmentally sound with late-twentieth century technology to protect materials from the harmful elements enumerated in 1940 by Fall. And, the facilities are expandable. As it now stands, the building area is 130,000 square feet, with an average shelving density of 55 volumes per square foot. Collection growth space availability still exceeds 20%. Although it is unlikely that many of CRL's library materials will be converted to or available in electronic formats soon, the building facilities are adequate to store its materials indefinitely.

Land adjacent to CRL's completed building modules will accommodate two more modules that would double the current square footage. With another building expansion, CRL could again enlarge its acceptance of printed volumes deposited by member libraries with local space shortages.

## Technology Overcomes Distance Barriers for Access and Delivery

CRL's cooperative collection program continues to benefit from the use of evolving technology: there is improved communications because of dynamically updated catalogs of library holdings available via the Internet; correspondence between CRL as a supplier of materials and requesters is improved by email and online interlibrary loan systems; and delivery of requested items is expedited by premium shipping services and electronic document delivery.

Researchers now have easy Internet access to global bibliographic information; they know that the universe of information available to them is no longer confined by their local library building. And more and more often, librarians are able to meet the expectations of a patron who sees a catalog record describing an item in a collection anywhere in the world and wants to examine the material within a brief timeframe. As the physical location of an item becomes less of a barrier to its accessibility, users are overcoming perceived barriers to full utilization of CRL: a researcher begins to think of CRL as a resource that can be contacted from his or her office and from which material is quickly delivered rather than as a library in Chicago.

## *CRL Provides the Framework and Human Resources for Problem Solving*

CRL was established to be a solution to a variety of issues facing libraries in higher education in the first half of the century. Today, as well as being the physical location where many programs are implemented, CRL is a forum for the process of problem solving.

The CRL of today and the future is not solely the organization's governing board or administration or staff–it is also the faculty and librarians and staff associated with member institutions who contribute their intellectual resources. CRL is not a storage library, it is a *managed* collection; and it is the members who are the stewards of the program. The specialized bibliographic skills among member library staffs and faculty subject expertise inform CRL's collection development decisions. The membership is and will continue to be the source for creative ways to keep CRL's program working and valuable in a changing world of scholarly communication.

## NOTES

1. Ernest C. Colwell, then Distinguished Visiting Professor at Emory University and consultant to the Fund on the Advancement of Education of the Ford Foundation,

speaking October 5, 1951, at the Midwest Interlibrary Center (MILC); in "Inter-university co-operation," *Library quarterly*, v.22, no.1, (Jan.1952):1-4.

2. John Fall. *A Proposal for a middle west deposit library.* [New York, 1940] Illinois Secretary of State.

3. *Articles of Incorporation under the General not for Profit Corporation Act for the Midwest Inter-Library Corporation, March 4, 1949.*

# Cooperative Collection Management: Online Discussion

Milton T. Wolf

**SUMMARY.** The online discussion, among some of the more capable practitioners, about the trials and tribulations of cooperative collection development brought forth an amazing number if insightful comments that should broaden the scope of understanding for anyone interested in the current state of collection development and management problems/solutions. While the concept of "local control" is not diminished, it is apparent (to these practitioners at least) that a self-sufficient research collection is both an oxymoron and an anachronism. Cooperative sharing of resources is the future! *[Article copies available for a fee from The Haworth Document Delivery Service: 1-800-342-9678. E-mail address: getinfo@haworthpressinc.com]*

For its Fiftieth Anniversary celebration, The Center for Research Libraries decided to host an online discussion about cooperative collection development. The following was posted to several listservs:

This is an invitation to participate in an online Discussion concerning collection development issues regarding research institutions: cooperation, collaboration, partnering. This discussion will

---

Milton T. Wolf is Vice President for Collection Programs at the Center for Research Libraries. He is also both a scholar and teacher of science fiction. He was founding editor of *Technicalities*, coeditor of *Thinking Robots, an Aware Internet, and Cyberpunk Librarians*, of a special issue on "The Information Future" in *Information Technology and Libraries*, of the 1996 science fiction anthology *Visions of Wonder* (New York: Tor), of *Information Imagineering: Meeting at the Interface*, and editor of a 1997 special issue of Shaw: *Shaw and Science Fiction* (Penn State University Press). He is also co-author of *Budgeting for Information Access* (ALA, 1998).

[Haworth co-indexing entry note]: "Cooperative Collection Management: Online Discussion." Wolf, Milton T. Co-published simultaneously in *Collection Management* (The Haworth Press, Inc.) Vol. 23, No. 4, 1998, pp. 59-93; and: *Cooperative Collection Development: Significant Trends and Issues* (ed: Donald B. Simpson) The Haworth Press, Inc., 1998, pp. 59-93. Single or multiple copies of this article are available for a fee from The Haworth Document Delivery Service [1-800-342-9678, 9:00 a.m. - 5:00 p.m. (EST). E-mail address: getinfo@haworthpressinc. com].

© 1998 by The Haworth Press, Inc. All rights reserved.

take place Online December 1-14, 1997. It will be hosted by The Center For Research Libraries and moderated by Milton T. Wolf, Vice President for Collection Programs at CRL.

We hope to bring forward the very best thinking on this subject and so we are asking anyone who is interested to provide us before December 1st with a one page abstract summarizing your view, experiences, recommendations, analyses, etc. of the issues associated with cooperative collection development.

Some of the possible issues:

1. Why cooperate?
2. Interlocking, yet independent collections?
3. Methodology of cooperation
4. Cost effectiveness
5. Budget sharing
6. Priorities
7. Ownership/access
8. Document delivery systems
9. Potential partners

We at The Center for Research Libraries believe that "the art of cooperation requires librarians' ability to comprehend and support big picture goals and the skills to incorporate common good objectives into local activities so that there is constructive and affirmative benefit to one's own programs and services." We hope you will join us in this discussion.

The following participants joined the discussion:

- Barbara McFadden Allen (BA), CIC Center for Library Initiatives, Director.
- Stephen J. Bensman (SB), Special Projects Librarian, Louisiana State University.
- Dan Hazen (DH), Harvard College Library, Librarian for Latin America, Spain and Portugal.
- Deborah L. Jakubs (DJ), Duke University, Head, International Area Studies Department.
- Susan Rabe (SR), The Center for Research Libraries, Collection Resources Bibliographer.

- Don Simpson (DS), The Center for Research Libraries, President.
- Geoff Smith (GS), British Library, Head of Modern Collections.
- GladysAnn Wells (GA), Arizona State Department of Library, Archives and Public Records, Director.
- E. Paige Weston [EPW], Illinois Library Computer Systems Office, Library Systems Coordinator.
- Stanley Wilder (SW), Louisiana State University, Assistant Dean for Technical and Financial Services.
- Milton T. Wolf (MW), The Center for Research Libraries, Vice President for Collection Programs.

To initiate the discussion I sent a note out addressed to "Partners," admittedly hoping to enflame some response, stating that we as profession pay a lot of lip service to the concept of cooperation, but when it comes right down to it, we banner it about, like "Mother and apple pie," as a way of convincing funding authorities to give us grants; and, if successful with this ploy, we fulfill the requirements of the grant and then we go on our own sweet way, reverting to the traditional position of building a self-sufficient, local collection.

Of course, I knew this was not entirely true as there have been some significant and partially successful attempts at shared collection development over the years, but I hoped to lure someone into the discussion. Thankfully, Deborah Jakubs (Duke University), who immediately saw through my ruse, graciously decided to help me get the "chat" launched with her following response:

[DJ:]
*Thanks for launching the discussion. One of the areas that I am most concerned about, from the perspective of what we are trying to do within the Global Resources Program, is how to actually bring about RELIANCE on other people/collections. We do, as you say, pay lip service to cooperation, but when it comes down to it, many people (and I think I mean bibliographers in this particular context) cannot cancel titles or stop collecting in some areas and rely on others to provide those materials to their patrons. I have thought a great deal about this, and observed a lot over the years (beginning with the early 1980s when I was managing the Conspectus at RLG and the issue of TRUST was a regular topic in the resource-sharing context), and it*

*seems that there are several things going on. One is that as bibliographers we do not like to disappoint our users, by telling them, e.g., that the gap in our collection is a CONSCIOUS gap. Another is that universities and libraries pride themselves on supporting their faculty and students, and for someone to tell a new faculty member (for instance) that s/he will expect to get most of his/her materials via document delivery/ILL may reflect badly on how that person and his or her work are regarded within the university. Another big issue is, of course, the relative speed of document delivery and ILL–can we in good faith tell faculty that having something elsewhere is just about as good as having it in their own library? Not if the turnaround time is a couple of weeks. So there are a number of built-in obstacles to really truly well-functioning cooperative collection development that are tough to get around. Can we?*

*I throw that to the group to discuss.*

Indeed, Deborah made several cogent points regarding the difficulty of cooperative collection development endeavors, and certainly one of the most important ones is how does a group go about developing "trust" that the other members will actually fulfill their obligations to the group. This is especially problematic because funding for library materials changes frequently (and often downward), sometimes several times during a fiscal year, leaving an otherwise committed participant without funds to carry out the contract to which they originally, whole-heartedly agreed.

And Deborah's point about the continued inadequacy of the speed of interlibrary loan as a method of sharing independent but interlocked collections foils many of librarians' "best laid plans" for cooperation. The most recent study of interlibrary loan by the Association of Research Libraries dolefully concludes that while interlibrary loan transactions have risen over 50 percent during the past decade, the turnaround time of two weeks remains the same–even with all the technological advances that have occurred!

Stephen J. Bensman then responded to Deborah Jakubs:

[SB:]
*In response to what Deborah Jakubs wrote, I think that things would become clearer, if one would divide materials into those for which cooperative collection development is an option and those for which it is not. In general, cooperative collection development is NOT an option for those materials which are high use, needed by every-*

*body, do not impact heavily the fixed costs of the library, or are within the historical strengths of the library. Cooperative collection development is also NOT an option for low use, high cost serials which impact the fixed costs of the library. For these, document delivery is best. Cooperative collection development IS an option for areas such as monographs on Kazakh or Armenian literature which do not impact fixed costs and can be divvied up among universities according to the collection priorities of those participating in the cooperative program.*

While some might argue with Stephen's contention that cooperative collection development is "not" an option for low use, high cost serials as opposed to document delivery, most institutions would agree with him that peripheral materials "are" likely candidates; however, that said, it is becoming increasingly clear that with the downsizing of university library material budgets, more and more research collections are beginning to look a lot alike. This homogenization may indicate a need to set aside some of the monies used for "high use" materials to contribute toward some shared collection of diverse materials.

Barbara McFadden Allen then weighed in with:

[BA:]
*Thanks, Deborah and Milton for the jumpstart. Let me add a couple of my own thoughts–and believe me these are my own thoughts, not necessarily representative of my CIC colleagues. I agree that we need stronger bibliographic and delivery systems that will effectively support cooperative collection management. However, isn't it true that one is often faced with fairly primitive and slow access to collections within our own campuses? I'm thinking here of situations in which the campus libraries operate as independent from the "main" library. I've had a sneaking suspicion that this objection (ILL takes two weeks) is sometimes used as a smokescreen. But let me repeat–we need stronger delivery systems and we should devote considerable attention to resolving this.*

*And, we know of the significant objections to cooperative collection management raised by our own staffs–but do we have anything except anecdotal evidence to document user concerns and frustrations? I readily admit the depth of my ignorance, and it is entirely possible that an entire body of literature has escaped my notice. Such a definition of concerns might help us focus action and address concerns of our staffs and users alike. Too, we may have all been looking at this the wrong way. Instead of 'forcing' cooperation as a means of proscribing certain behaviors, perhaps we should promote it in a "bigger picture" sense. That is, if we can solve the problems of delivery (which appear solvable, by the way) can't we set up collaboration that allows you–authorizes you–not to have to collect in certain areas? Isn't that, after all, what we do when we rely on CRL for certain materials. And, by allowing bibliographers and subject specialists to address problems collaboratively, it has been my experience that they typically come up with some pretty good–though non-threatening–ideas (e.g., collaborative web page development, shared serials lists). Once relationships and projects are established, the notion of greater dependence upon one another is not as threatening and substantial projects can blossom. As a matter of fact, two of our universities have elected to actually "share" a bibliographer who will oversee the development of complementary collections on each campus.*

*Finally, I think that the shift from paper to a mix of digital and traditional collections will focus our attention on cooperation if for no other reason than the obvious–we cannot support full scale development of both "kinds" of libraries (the paper and the digital) with current funds. The price differences on reference materials alone are breathtaking! Thus, even those librarians who have rejected CCD [cooperative collection development] may see it as an essential tool in providing access to the potential universe of publication.*

*Looking forward to further lively debate on these issues.*

Barbara's point about getting librarians to see a "bigger picture" than their own library is essential if truly national/international cooperation is to flourish and begin to provide a more varied menu of information options to the research communities' clientele–which, to a significant degree, has been put on a "core" diet of homogeneous materials.

Her intuition that the ongoing shift to digital materials will help us adjust our attitudes to cooperative endeavors is an important one because as we become more accustomed to accessing material rather than 'owning' it, we may lose some of our traditional reluctance to sharing.

Also, Barbara's testimony about sharing bibliographers is one that could be done at many other institutions (although with the caveat that Deborah Jakubs makes in a later response). Tied together as many of us are by e-mail, the process not only of sharing bibliographers but also of doing online cooperative collection development seems feasible and desirable in certain instances. If we can only grasp the fact that whether we know it or not, all libraries are building a worldwide collection right now–only rather poorly!

Stephen Bensman again joined in, only this time with his colleague Stanley Wilder (Assistant Dean for Technical and Financial Services), to present the following:

[SB and SW:]
*Cooperative collection development is not a viable option in respect to scientific/technical serials. This conclusion is based on the overall functioning of the scientific/technical serials system. The scientific/ technical serials system and the social stratification system of science/ technology on which it is based appear to operate on the same probability structure as that of biological nature and society. This probability structure is dominated by highly skewed, stable distributions arising from two interactive stochastic processes, inhomogeneity and contagion. The result is the creation of a scientific/technical elite, which centers around a few traditionally prestigious institutions and publishes generally in US association journals. Due to this phenomenon, US association journals have a higher scientific/technical value and can be sold to libraries in greater numbers at a cheaper price. In contrast, the serials of the commercial publishers have a lesser scientific/technical value, can be sold in lesser numbers, and therefore must have a higher price to cover first copy costs.*

*The consequence is a bifurcated scientific/technical serials market with scientific/technical value concentrating on the titles of the US associations and costs on the titles of the commercial publishers.*

*As a result of their higher scientific/technical value, US association serials play a dominant role not only in internal library usage but also in interlibrary loan. Studies done by the National Library of Medicine in the late 1950s, Chemical Abstracts Service in the 1960s, as well as the British Library Lending Division in the 1970s and 1980s have shown that the same journals tend to dominate both internal library and interlibrary usage. Moreover, other studies have also shown that journals not used internally tend also not to be borrowed through interlibrary loan. This is primarily a function of all libraries acting as part of the same social stratification system and requiring basically the same set of journals.*

*Evidence of these phenomena was found in a recent study of scientific/technical serials at Louisiana State University (LSU). This study analyzed UnCover document deliveries to LSU, revealing the crucial role played in these by serials highly ranked by the LSU faculty and citation measures. Moreover, there were also found high intercorrelations among LSU faculty ratings, total SCI citations, and University of Illinois at Urbana-Champaign (UIUC) library usage in chemistry, and this finding showed that LSU and UIUC functioned as part of the same social stratification system and needed basically the same set of serials in this discipline.*

*The final argument against cooperative collection development for scientific/technical serials is provided by studies which found that those low in scientific/serial value but high in cost are most prone to be canceled by libraries. Such serials are not only high in cost due to their low value preventing their sale in large numbers but are also subject to inflationary pressure due to an ever shrinking subscription base from cancellations. Therefore cooperative collection development would saddle libraries with highly priced serials with high inflation rates and little probability of being borrowed either locally or through interlibrary loan.*

*A far better solution would be some system of document delivery, which would enable libraries both to rationalize their cost structures and force the demise of numerous expensive, secondary scientific/technical serials through free market pressures.*

Bensman and Wilder tackled what is certainly one of the most egregious problems confronting libraries today: the high cost of scientific journals. While numerous papers have been written on this subject, we still find ourselves unable to fulfill locally the demands that science has thrust upon us. Part of the problem is the Publisher/Government/Sciences Complex which has created an incestuous relationship that generates more and more data, less and less competition and a virtual monopoly on scientific publication and research. About 75 percent of U.S. titles are published by approximately 2 percent of the publishers! And European scientific publishing is dominated by what can only be called a behemoth monopoly.

Dan Hazen was next to join the fray with a well thought-out synopsis and list of insightful questions for us to pursue:

[DH:]
*It seems to me that our discussion so far has identified several dimensions relevant to cooperative collection development, albeit in some cases only implicitly. These topics include trust, politics, use, cost, mechanics and logistics, formats, disciplines or fields, and cost/ benefit calculations. I wonder whether, while recognizing the connections among all of these, we might try carving up the discussion in hopes of greater focus. To that end, here's a sample sequence of questions for your comment:*

*I. What is cooperative collection development?–How explicit must it be? [Some would argue that reporting requirements for preservation microfilm masters amount to an implicit arrangement for cooperative collection development of a national/international collection of preserved materials. Others would say that these arrangements only allow for nonduplicative filming, and can't really qualify as "cooperation."]*

*–Does it subsume document delivery? [Stephen and Stanley suggest that document delivery is a different animal from cooperative collection development. Others say cooperative collection building assumes access arrangements, i.e., effective document delivery.]*

*–Does it mean the same thing for all formats (and especially for both electronic and hardcopy materials)? [One can argue that access/"document delivery" functions are taken care of with networked electronic resources–though licensing and authorization restrictions can become primary. Are the issues surrounding electronic materials enough like those associated with print to consider them together?]*

*II. Why engage in cooperative collection development?*
*–Are we seeking to cut costs? Do we expect savings in acquisitions alone, or for the library as a whole? Is the appropriate frame of reference–for cost savings or anything else–the single library, a network/consortium of institutions, or specific scholarly communities and their access to information?–Do we want to broaden access to information?–Are we looking at cost/benefit calculations?*

*–Do we seek intangible benefits (such as becoming known as cooperative innovators or team players, in contrast with self-sufficient elitists)?–Will all potential partners in cooperative collection development share a single set of criteria for success? What if they don't?*

*III. What are the models for cooperative collection development, and their benefits and drawbacks? How have different organizational, administrative, and funding structures worked out over time?–Distributed systems, in which many libraries share responsibility for acquisitions and for guaranteeing intellectual and physical access to the materials.–Consortially funded institutions, like CRL, supported by many participants.–De facto leaders, like the Library of Congress.–Commercial/non-commercial service agencies, like document delivery providers.*

I regret that I'm extremely pressed for time these days, so I can't continue right now. I'll welcome reactions, and hope to be back before too long!--

There were so many possibilities to pursue in Dan's response that I decided to single out just one: *You laid out enough for me to cogitate on for the rest of the week:-) Was especially interested in your question: Do we really want to increase access? What exactly did you have in mind there?*

[DH:]
*We're drilled, from the time that we're cub librarians, that our mission and our business are to provide information as quickly and efficiently and freely as possible. Anything that limits access, by this ideology, is somewhere between a necessary evil (usually rooted in logistics or procedures) and a straight-out Sin. You can't have too much of either apple pie or access.*

*The picture shifts, however, as concrete situations come into play. Many major libraries have been built because their parent institutions considered them critical. The institutional resources required to create strong collections have come from student fees, endowments, and allocations by the college or university. These collections exist, first and foremost, to serve the needs of local students and faculty. The needs of these groups, then, are (arguably) not met if local materials are indis-*

*criminately available to (and away at) students and scholars at other institutions.*

*Quite apart from whether cooperative collecting arrangements include mechanisms to cover the real costs of interlibrary loan/document delivery for each institution (on which more below), an item on loan to another library is not available for the primary constituency of local users for whom it was acquired and who, directly or indirectly, paid for it. If access is too broad, the library stands to hinder rather than help the local users it was created to serve.*

*This eases the issue toward considerations of the specific circumstances in which cooperative collection development–assuming reliability and trust and full cost recovery mechanisms–makes sense for a library. For cooperative collection development, defined as distributed collecting and resource sharing, there may need to be a rough parity among participants. A very large collection simply stands to experience too much demand on materials in the first instance acquired for local users if its cooperative partners are all relatively small repositories with little more than core collections. Yes, I'm sure that every library has some holdings that are unique. But I doubt that effective collections cooperation can happen if partners are wildly disparate in terms of the size and scope of their collections, precisely because the stronger institutions will no longer be able to provide an expected level of access to their local constituents.*

*Defining "strong collections," and the potential circles of partners for distributed cooperative collection development, then becomes a matter to be worked out discipline by discipline, field by field. This suggests a mosaic of cooperative arrangements and agreements within each institution which, in turn, may drive interlibrary loan/document delivery staffs to happy early retirements.*

*Cycling back, distributed cooperative collection development and interlibrary loan/document delivery will–quite apart from considerations of when demands for broadened access (or, phrasing it another way, for the reduced availability of local collections) become unacceptably high–require a means to recover all the transaction costs. These range all over the place, for reasons both obvious and not. Everyone recognizes that salary levels and real estate costs vary among regions. The sheer size of a library also has a direct impact on cost: I have to allow about 20 minutes every time I want to duck into our stacks to locate a book. If it's housed in off-site storage, there's a* one-day wait (plus a real cash retrieval charge absorbed by the library). This means that it costs Harvard a lot just to locate an item, quite apart from the subsequent expenses of the ILL sequence. Retrieval stands to be far quicker, and cheaper, at a smaller place. Cooperation, in this real-world scenario, won't work by finding an average ILL transaction cost and then applying it across the board: every institution's real expenses need to be met. (I also think that ILL charges SHOULD, even though they generally don't, also include some sort of surcharge for preservation.)

There may be analogies here to levels of access considered "appropriate" for other kinds of university facilities–say, scientific labs or football stadiums. Institution-based exotic scientific equipment, even when acquired (as is often the case) through external grants, is customarily limited to those associated with the institution and/or the research project. (I think the model is somewhat different for multi-institution facilities, like some astronomical observatories–which seem more analogous to the "CRL model" within librarianship.) Those users have preferential access to the equipment, and outsiders may not be allowed at all. Likewise, if a university decides that its best investment is in a sports facility [as opposed to a library–for shame!! ... ], then–customarily–university teams have priority in using the facility. Outsiders, if allowed in at all, will have to pay. In other words, universities are chock-full of resources and services which everyone expects to be off-limits to outsiders. It's not clear why the same sort of reasoning shouldn't apply to libraries. In other words: broadened access is by no means a self-evident goal. We rather need to engage in close analysis of when, why, and how it makes sense.

Some of these arguments shift if the cooperative model moves from distributed collecting and resource sharing to common support for a separate institution (a la CRL). In that instance, other costs and benefits come into play. Though that's for another day ...

I wanted the group's thoughts on Dan's feeling that some parity is needed among institutions if they are going to find a basal line of cooperation, so I queried them:

[MW:]
*I would be interested in what any of you might add here to Dan's thoughts. Is equal parity a sine qua non for effective cooperation?*

And much of what Deborah said made me ask if she wasn't suggesting, in an era in which "content" has become paramount in collection building, that more bibliographers were needed in libraries:

[MW:]
*I think that one of the things that could be construed from your remarks is that a truly integrated cooperative effort would require more bibliographers, not less. Should we, then, be pushing harder for more recruitment of bibliographers?*

At this point the online chat went off simultaneously in several directions, but it continued to relate back to what had been said earlier by the various respondents. For the sake of a linear reading I edited these divergent conversations as though they were strictly chronological.

Deborah disagreed with both Barbara and me about sharing bibliographers:

[DJ:]
*Well . . . I do not support sharing bibliographers, except perhaps in extreme cases, and certainly not when there are, on both campuses, a significant number of faculty and a significant academic program in whatever area you're sharing in. I can see if you have a strong program/ weak program relationship and the weak institution wouldn't have a bibliographer at all otherwise. But I think the idea of sharing is a dangerous one, because it doesn't take into consideration the full spectrum of responsibilities and roles that a subject specialist plays on a campus. Book selection is a relatively small chunk of how we spend our time–a lot more is spent providing specialized research assistance, participating in program development, assisting with language/subject questions from tech services, and writing or helping to write grant proposals. I am especially aware of this from all the work that has been stimulated by the Indiana University conferences on the Future of Area Librarianship. It is also my understanding that the CIC experiment with sharing a South Asian bibliographer has not really been deemed a true success.*

[MW:]
*Again, your points are well taken. A bibliographer is going to have plenty to keep him/her busy in terms of interaction with the users, and there is a danger in "watering down" bibliographers' workloads so that one can easily get the wrong idea about what a bibliographer is/can be.*

However, for many institutions who cannot yet afford bibliographers, this could be a way to get a foot in the door, and perhaps show how valuable they could be. Also, when a bibliographer works with two (or more) collections at different institutions, the amount of cooperation would seemingly have to increase–not to mention that the collections should be much more congruent.

Of course, it would have to be constantly stressed that a shared bibliographer is not as good as one devoted, full time to one collection.

I think that one of the things that could be construed from your remarks is that a truly integrated cooperative effort would require more bibliographers, not less. Should we, then, be pushing harder for more recruitment of bibliographers?

[DJ:]

It is clear that a lot of intellectual effort needs to go into designing projects (such as those encompassed by the Global Resources Program) that will truly address the scholarly needs of a field and make sense within the library context–and within an international context, if relevant. So I see the role of the bibliographer/subject specialist to be very important here, not only in the design phase but in the implementation and continued monitoring and evaluation of the projects as well. Whether that means we need MORE bibliographers or just need to maintain the number we have at the institutions with serious collections. I think this issue goes hand-in-hand with the uphill battle we seem to keep having to fight to explain to people that bibliographers really DO DO things other than select books from catalogs. That is an old-fashioned view of the world that doesn't consider Web development, Internet resources, outreach, etc., etc. And the management of cooperative programs is one of the newer aspects of the job of the bibliographer (do we need a different term?). We have certainly seen it in the Latin American project, multiplied by the 38 member libraries! In these online discussions we have also touched on the topic of changing the faculty culture. I think that the bibliographer, one-on-one, stands the best chance of bringing this about by engaging faculty in discussion of resource-sharing projects and explaining to them that cooperative collection development is not meant to LIMIT their access but in fact to broaden it, as we are able collectively to capture more publications/information in our libraries. There is a lot of discussion *of how to get faculty involved and informed, and it has been my experience that having a "personal librarian" (like a personal banker or personal trainer??) goes a long way to improve things.*

Deborah's concept of a "personal bibliographer" struck a chord with several of us. With the emphasis finally shifting to the "content" of the library and not the number of books it contains, many of us realize that librarians have been so busy doing other things that they have almost given up "selecting" along the lines of what constitutes valuable additions to scholarship. Blanket ordering, approval ordering (unless monitored very closely), and reduced acquisition funds have made bibliographers very rare birds indeed. Those teaching faculty lucky enough to have personal bibliographers realize the value of having someone who actually knows their field of research.

Stephen replied: *"Personal bibliographer? All faculty members want a personal bibliographer-one with plenty of money who will do and buy anything they want. I want a personal bibliographer."*

Stephen then went on to address my question: What would be the best forum for engaging the faculty and raising consciousness of this issue?

[SB:]
*I am afraid that there is no forum for engaging the faculty. The interests of librarians and faculty are diametrically opposed. Librarians are under extreme pressure to keep their budgets in balance and purchase fairly for all disciplines. Faculty are under extreme pressure to publish and need an ever increasing serials universe. History has shown that there are no peaceful solutions under such conditions. That is why so much money has been made in the production of weapons. Librarians will be compelled to rationalize their cost structures by cancellations and new ways of delivering scientific/technical information in the face of opposition of faculty and publishers. The faculty have more interests in common with the publishers than with librarians. I'm sorry to be so pessimistic. Anybody going into collection development is a fool.*

[DJ:]
*I guess I am not as cynical as Stephen Bensman. Or maybe I am a fool because I am in collection development? I have a very different view of*

*things, particularly of faculty and their needs/wants/demands/desires. I think this is due in part to the fact that I am someone with a foot on either side of the fence, so to speak, since I serve as the Director of the Duke-University of North Carolina Program in Latin American Studies and as such spend a lot of time with faculty in a somewhat different capacity than when I am doing my library work. I have found that while it may be true that some faculty do not pay attention to library issues until and unless they affect something they care deeply about, it is equally true that librarians ASSUME that faculty know a lot more about library things than they do–and so I have seen over and over again that librarians get upset when faculty don't read their minds, when in fact they simply don't have enough information about a given issue–and it is up to US to give that information to them, not simply to assume that they are bad and selfish because they do not see things our way.*

*This gets into another topic that really doesn't belong here, but I will mention it, at least in passing: the insecurity of librarians and how that affects their relationships with faculty. We have a lot to give in terms of information and assistance that takes many forms, and yet many librarians seem to be stuck in their own minds in the shadow of faculty, and moan and groan about it. The information sharing and mutual participation in working toward solving library/scholarly communication problems that we so want to happen will not happen if librarians come from a position of weakness.*


[MW:]
*I agree that I often encounter this "position of weakness" concerning librarians and teaching faculty. Part of it stems, I guess, from our support role, but I have noticed over years that as I taught more I was accepted more–and tended to be listened to more. And, as I published in more respected journals, I found myself receiving more invitations to guest lecture.*

*Obviously, if librarians were more collegial with the teaching faculty, more common concerns could be more easily explored. Since not every librarian is going to be able to teach and publish because there are so many tasks which we do to keep libraries running, how do we bridge this gap? Are there any associations that could help? Do we need to think about creating such an association?*

[DJ:]
*Milton et al.,*

*I don't think that one has to actively publish and be a "pseudo faculty member" to be appreciated and to make a contribution. It's fine, and nice, if you do, but what faculty really need and want is someone who is knowledgeable about a field and able to help them find their way through the mass of information that is out there. This includes being on the lookout for new books and resources that may be of interest. I have had this debate with one of the members of my department, who believes rather adamantly that doing research (on the job) is a critically important part of his job because it makes the faculty respect him; meanwhile, the faculty tell ME that they wish he would spend more time being a librarian and helping them in unique ways–that is what THEY say builds respect.*

The group then circled back to Stephen J. Bensman and Stanley Wilder's earlier position that favors document delivery for certain materials.

[MW:]
*Your last sentence is intriguing: "A far better solution would be some system of document delivery, which would enable libraries both to rationalize their cost structures and force the demise of numerous expensive, secondary scientific/technical serials through free market pressures."*

*Aren't you indicating then that a "cooperative" approach is still necessary and needed? Also, couldn't the cooperative effort be launched around collecting only the primary materials and sharing them, while letting the secondary materials die a capitalist death of non-purchase? Of course, the faculties of these institutions would have to agree on what is primary and secondary, so more cooperative interactions would need to take place.*

[SB:]
*Our main concern is scientific/technical serials. It is here that there is occurring the explosion in fixed costs which is crippling libraries. This area of libraries is rapidly moving into cyberspace. For example, the American Chemical Society now has all of its journals online. The transfer to cyberspace is now technologically feasible and will occur*

rapidly. The only argument is on what socioeconomic conditions will this transfer take place.

It is time for libraries to abandon the subscription system and go to the free market. Under conditions of the subscription system cooperative collection development is not a feasible option for libraries, for reasons mentioned. However, libraries will need to cooperate in some form to create a free market. Having considered all the options, the free market seems the fairest, since it will equalize costs among all libraries. The real cost of a scientific/technical serial is cost-per-use, and, needless to say, larger institutions with larger usage have cheaper cost-per-use. I was at the last conference of the American Chemical Society (ACS). Here I heard a lot of complaints by small Texas colleges, who were being forced to cooperate to buy ACS journals to be accredited by the ACS. Their usage does not justify full subscription prices, and they should have the opportunity to buy only what they need at fair prices. But for this to happen there has to be created a free market by all libraries through some sort of cooperation.

I am in correspondence with an ACS Chief Technical Officer, who has made the transfer from paper to the electronic journal. He is most concerned about archiving. For example, the Chemical Abstracts Service discards issues which are older than 20 years. This cannot be made a universal rule for the sake of human knowledge, and libraries must step in to fill the gap by undertaking their historic archival role. However, all this requires some sort of planning and cooperation–to create a library in cyberspace accessible to anybody anywhere. This can only be done in cooperation, but I do not know how it will occur–whether libraries in cooperation, the government, or private companies will do it.

When the free market has been created, the cost of information will become rational as documents will have to be produced with the calculation that they will have to be used to pay their way. What will happen in science/technology will happen in other areas. For example, IBM is digitalizing the Vatican Library, and LSU Libraries has digitalized Louisiana newspapers. Others are doing the same. We are living in an age equivalent to the one from the invention of the printing press to the invention of the scientific journal, but instead of 200 years we will do it in 20 or less.

I would like to clarify the distinction between cooperative collection development and document delivery. With cooperative collection de-

*velopment a group of libraries divvy up resources, each agreeing to hold a share and assume a financial burden. With document delivery, some outside source–a company, central library like the British Library Document Supply Centre–supplies the documents, while the libraries only buy from the source as needed. In the latter case the libraries assume no financial burden until the purchase of the document, and the risk is allocated to the outside source. The matter is going to get complicated, because with information going into cyberspace, there may only be some central pool from which everybody draws documents as needed, and libraries as physical entities may disappear. At that point we are dealing with a free market in information, and the economics of information radically changes. My mind boggles at the complexities of this thing. Who will have archival responsibilities? etc.? I hope this clarifies our distinction between cooperative collection development and document delivery.*

[MW:]

*I'm still a little fuzzy on "how?" libraries could create the free market. Do you think if The Center for Research Libraries approached the American Chemical Society with an offer to "archive" their publications, they would then commit themselves to permitting research libraries to access their electronic files on a need-only basis? for a reasonable fee?*

*In a truly free market are there monopolies, like the American Chemical Society? It would seem that if they both give the imprimatur of accreditation, but only if you hold a significant portion of their publications, then they have a monopolistic hold on the academic world. Not to mention that "publish or perish" helps foster a publishing empire that has more interest in the bottom line than in research.*

*If libraries abandon the subscription system, especially to scientific publications, exactly how do you see libraries cooperating toward a free market? What steps need to be taken?*

*Any ideas that will get us out of our present bind are welcome: sometimes the utopian approach is the only one remaining.*

[DH:]

*So is the Center for Research Libraries, where a group of libraries each allocates resources to a central entity that they in some sense "own," and who jointly define collection development policies, an example of cooperative collection development? I'd say it is, though I don't think your definition would allow it.*

[SB:]

*I am not clear myself on how the free market will be created. But there are already forces working in this direction. For example, private companies like UnCover and the Institute for Scientific Information are either offering or ready to start offering document delivery. Then there is the Chemical Abstract Services document delivery system of the ACS. The model library for document delivery is the British Library Document Supply Centre, whose name change from the British Library Lending Division emphasizes its new concept of mission. Perhaps the free market will just evolve, but there seems to be a need for libraries to undertake some cooperative planning to make sure that the archival function is fulfilled in the electronic age. Right now I am doing research which requires me to read statistical papers written in the period 1890-1943.*

*I would like to address the concept of "monopoly" which seems to captivate librarians trained in an era of heavy Marxist influence. I fail to see the effects of monopoly. The publishers with the most monopoly powers due to the absolute need of their products–i.e., the US associations–charge the least amount of money for these products. Regression analyses have consistently shown that in the case of all types of publishers–association and commercial, domestic and foreign–price consistently goes down as the number of library subscriptions goes up. The most expensive titles can be canceled with the least loss in scientific value. Where is the monopoly power? The problem may lie more in the inability of librarians to manage their collections properly due to their value systems, ignorance, and fear of the faculty. It is politically easier to scapegoat the publishers as greedy monopolists than to face the ire of the faculty protecting their publication outlets. The problem is not greedy monopolists but a system gone dysfunctional. It is the system that needs changing–to one that is self-governing and less subject to political pressures. But the change will not come easy, given that powerful forces have vested interests in the existing system.*

Extract: *"It is politically easier to scapegoat the publishers as greedy monopolists than to face the ire of the faculty protecting their publication outlets."*

[MW:]
*I think there is a lot of truth here. ARL has found a similar dilemma in trying to convince teaching/publishing faculty that they need to make common cause with librarians in order to escape the present system of being unable to purchase the ever-increasing number of publications at ever-increasing prices.*

GladysAnn Wells, Director of the Arizona State Department of Library, Archives and Public Records, then joined the online discussion with:

[GA:]
Hello Milton et al.,
*I think the most exciting aspect of cooperation is just now being realized–the numerous statewide contracts for books, journals and databases being developed across the country represent a more positive step than we have enjoyed in the past.*

[MW:]
*Your comment, GladysAnn, helps show how diverse the concept of cooperation is becoming: all types of information institutions, commercial vendors, quasi-governmental agencies are crossing lines and negotiating a varied assortment of proposals.*

[GA:]
*Let me share with you two paragraphs of an abstract of Merrill Distad's (Associate Director, University of Alberta Library) reflections on the difficulties of resource sharing in Canada that might stimulate some online discussion:*

1. As even the largest libraries have been forced to trim serials subscriptions, academic library collections, falling back upon the retention of "core" titles, have become more and more mirror-images of each other. This trend, combined with the difficulty of predicting budget cuts and forced cancellations, makes the coordination of any cooperative collection development plan that involves rationalization of holdings a challenge.
2. Finally, our experience suggests that other issues, such as institutional autonomy, budget sharing, and the like can be overcome once sufficient budgetary pressure and administrative deter-

*mination are brought to bear. Our experience, nearly a decade ago, in spearheading a consortial effort by more than forty Canadian libraries, to negotiate collectively for discounts with eight European journal publishers–an utterly Quixotic project, but one we felt bound to try–taught us that solutions to our collections budget problems must come at the library end, where we (and not the publishers) still exercise SOME degree of control. Optimists among us still hope to live to see the day when academics no longer are free to give away the copyrights to the fruit of their scholarly research.*

So far in these online discussions (and elsewhere), it appears that the kind of cooperation that libraries and librarians would like to enter into for the betterment of their clientele is being hampered/hindered by that very clientele! In particular, it seems more and more as if the teaching faculty need to be educated about their central role in the problem, about what appears to be an almost intransigent position on their part to do anything but complain. Since libraries and librarians are basically a service industry to the teaching faculty, any hope of changing the present situation would seem to require a significant educational thrust at the highest levels of the academic hierarchy. Otherwise, the hidden marriage between the teaching faculty and the publishing world could result in libraries being nothing more than limited repositories of their commercial progeny;-) The question of who actually directs research would then be rather apparent!

[SB:]
*Boy! Do I agree with those sentiments! Atta girl, GladysAnn! It seems I have found a soul mate.*

At this juncture Susan Rabe, Collection Resources Bibliographer at CRL, refocused us on Dan Hazens' earlier set of thoughts/questions regarding "just what is cooperative collection development?":

[SR:]
*I'd like to jump into the fray with a couple of thoughts in response to Dan Hazen's list of questions.*

*I wonder does cooperative collection development have anything to do with selection? Selection seems to be an integral part of the consortial model of cooperative collection development, especially as prac-*

*ticed in the digital environment. A group joins together to jointly purchase access to a particular digital product. Selection has also been important in some tests of distributed cooperative collection development such as the ARL Latin American project for serials but that is a relatively small and tightly defined case. BUT, I agree with Dan's opinion that local needs will continue to determine selection. If this is the case, then cooperative collection development is not about selection but about cooperating to build a collective collection by sharing information about what is in each collection (bibliographic access, union lists of serial holdings, copy information, etc.) and sharing physical access to those collections. This is Barbara Allen's point that cooperative collection development efforts should focus on the issues of access (bibliographic and physical) and delivery. I believe that efforts should be put toward eliminating these barriers that undermine user confidence in distributed collections to build the trust and reliance that Deborah Jakubs mentioned. If access and delivery are quick and painless to the user would we need to engage them in this discussion? Would they care where their needed materials were from?*

[MW:]

*Susan Rabe's point is well taken that "cooperative collection development is not about selection but cooperating to build a collective collection by sharing information about what is in each collection (bibliographic access, union lists of serial holdings, copy information, etc.) and sharing physical access to those collections."*

*And from the literature that I am familiar with, it suggests that most collections contain about twenty percent of unique materials. True: a lot of it is of local interest and often much is uncataloged (and in small libraries that are not often thought of as "research" institutions), but the point is that if we could focus on this unique material in a cooperative manner (grants, etc.), there are real possibilities of extending the access to research materials farther and wider than we have ever done before.*

*I think, also, that Susan's point that cooperative collection development doesn't have as much to do with selection (because it is so locally driven), but with how we go about sharing what we have (access, union lists, serial holdings) and delivery mechanisms.*

*Whether we believe it or not, we are really building a national/in-*

ternational collection. We might do it with more purpose if we but realize it. Over to you.

[DH:]
It's fascinating to watch our discussion of cooperation bounce around between mildly quixotic condemnations of the faculty (for and with whom we work, after all), clarion calls for stiff-backed militance vis-à-vis exploitative publishers (though presumably in manners that don't run afoul of restraint of trade legislation), and–above and through it all–doubts over where librarians can and should fit into the whole panorama. Are we really the consumers in this picture, or are we just representatives and proxies for the _real_ consumers, our scholars and students?

Much of the discussion seems to be centering on expensive (primarily scientific and technical) journals, since their price increases are both high and the most obvious threats to library budgets and collection depth. Stephen and Stanley's initial contribution focuses on this body of material, and suggests a (rather convenient) segmentation between cheaper and more useful titles, primarily published by [virtuous] academic societies and other non-profit agents; and more expensive and less useful titles that come from for-profit publishers. The proposed solution, which is essentially to boycott the expensive publications/publishers in order to bring supply into line with libraries' means (and hence the demand), would presumably both reinforce the values of scholarship divorced from profit and would restore our wayward researchers to purity of publishing purpose in a neatly self-contained academic superstructure.

I wonder what happens if the same sort of analysis is applied to other kinds of publications, perhaps those not so obviously expensive. In an area like Latin American Studies, one might well conclude–based on citation studies or other measures of use–that the most "valuable" titles are those published in English, in this country. The lesser-used, more expensive stuff–sometimes in terms of list price, but more often in terms of the extra processing required and the specialized staff needed to ensure usability–tends to come from abroad. In this case, the segmentation of the publishing market probably wouldn't coincide with a for-profit/non-profit split, but might rather suggest a differentiation associated with place of publication. Indulging the "free market" here, then, might simply mean writing off our international collections.

*I suspect that something like the "80-20" rule will apply to almost any bunch of library materials: only a small share of any universe of material will prove to be the most "useful" in terms of citations or loans or other likely measures. If the argument, however couched, boils down to saying libraries should ignore the "non-useful" stuff–because it's expensive, because the publishers make too much money off the sales, because it's just too damn obscure–then I think we're at danger of losing our mission and our purpose.*

*We probably need to take different tacks as we approach the very real crisis of escalating journal prices in science and technology on one hand, and as we examine other fields in which our aggregate coverage is inadequate. We can't act alone in any of these cases. I'm also far from sure that measures to ease the budget pressures in sci/ tech areas can really substitute for a broad range of cooperative collecting endeavors in many other fields. Wherever we act, we need to do so in tandem with the faculty. Wherever we act, too, we need to do so in full awareness of the entire structure of scholarly communication, and of the multiple relationships among all the players.*

Don Simpson then joined us:

[DS:]
*Hello all,*

*Let me jump in now that I am temporarily returned from travels everywhere.*

*I confess I agree with Deborah in that faculty are not clairvoyant. Most are reasonable when the facts are duly explained in terms they can process easily. However, I just attended an SSRC workshop in which one faculty member stated flatly that a suggestion that any part of journal pricing is market-driven is ludicrous because all journals from all publishers are priced solely on the realistic basis of recovering their huge investments in first-copy costs. I countered that this is true up to a point–true for "non-profit" journals and even somewhat true for European commercial journals in their first year of publication. If the publishers lowered their costs after they recoup their sunken investments, then it would be wholly true, but they don't out of fear. These publishers hang on for dear life to a product that is very late in its life cycle and they cannot see their way clearly to a replacement product.*

*This person went on to say that librarians' concerns about digitizing* retrospective collections and archiving electronic resources were unfounded as the commercial sector was already in control of the situation. He cited his belief that Xerox has announced it will make and sell no more photocopiers after 2005 since all important and useful literature will appear only in electronic format by then and Xerox will have reformatted all useful retrospective materials. (The implication is that with all documents readable online, printers and copiers are no longer needed.) He concluded with "how could a ten billion dollar corporation be wrong?" (I politely suggested he look at some corporate strategies put forward by IBM, Kodak, and General Motors in recent decades.)

Still, how do you approach the faculty? Carefully and with facts well in hand, of course. I believe we must reach them on campus as well as through their scholarly societies. Also, in deference to Stephen's clearly stated views, I want to note that dealing with these questions is very different for the humanities and area studies than for science and engineering. At CRL, we are able to provide cooperative collection development after a fashion for a lot of materials across a wide range of humanities; our options for science are much more limited for the reasons Stephen cites. As a result, CRL is more of a hybrid rather than clearly either a BLDSC or local cooperative collection development agency. Our current science journals are not the ones needed on campus everyday and while one might argue that the market should drive such journals to oblivion, as long as they do exist, CRL provides a relatively cheap and effective way of making them available to users. And, of course, there is the enduring question about making them permanently available even when no longer currently published. A true commercial model disallows maintaining an extensive inventory or even "parts" when demand declines considerably.

Enough for now. Comments?

[SB:]
I want to make several points both to answer what I have read from others and to clarify my position.

> 1. There seems to be some confusion in respect to first copy costs. First copy costs are not like an investment in a nuclear power plant, i.e., a one-shot affair which is then depreciated over time. First copy costs recur again and again for every issue of a journal. It is not a question of "virtuous" associations against

*"greedy" commercials. The simple fact of the matter is that the associations have better stuff, can sell more of it, and therefore can charge less for it. On the other hand, the commercials sell for the most part second-rate stuff, can't sell much of it, and have to charge much more to cover their first copy costs. For a good analysis of the dysfunctionality of the scientific/technical serials market, read the article by Noll and Steinmueller, two Stanford economists, in SERIALS REVIEW, Vol. 18 (1992), 32-37. If you want to see an application of the Noll/Steinmueller model, I can send you by e-mail the conclusion of our paper on the scientific/technical serials market.*
2. *Set definitions are all important in library science. Scientific journals are much different than Latin American materials and must be handled differently. In my mind, I have always divided disciplines into those which study reality and those which study books. The first–like science and many social sciences–require fast, up-to-date information readily retrievable. The latter–like the humanities and history–find their primary information in libraries, and nobody knows the importance of the stuff until some scholar discovers it. The first type of materials is amenable to usage and cost analysis, but the latter is not. The first type is not amenable to cooperative collection development; the latter is. The problem is that the information system for the first has gone dysfunctional and is squeezing out the second.*
3. *I am not advocating any policy. I am only describing what will have to happen due to the forces in play. Libraries will have to rationalize their cost structures, but this rationalization will threaten many professional and monetary interests. The system will be rationalized but at the cost of the careers of many librarians. Wars have been fought for reasons less clear than the ones affecting library purchasing power.*

*I hope this clarifies my thinking somewhat.*

[DS:]
*Stephen,*

*I suppose it is because I am not an economist that I have trouble seeing this as clearly as you do. You state it cogently and you are reshaping my opinions on this. It was Noll who made the "ludicrous" comment during the meeting I attended last weekend in Palo Alto.*

*While he may be correct, his arrogance detracted from his point. However, I will read his paper and I would like you to email me your paper, please.*

*So, if I read this accurately, librarians would have a chance to solve the STM journal "crisis" if faculty would stop publishing in these second-rate commercial journals, which could allow librarians to stop buying them, and they would die a natural death. Both librarians and faculty would therefore be better off if only the high-quality "association" journals continued to exist. Thus, at the root of the solution to the problem is the need to decouple P&T (promotion and tenure) from publishing.*

*How am I doing?*

[MW:]
*Partners:*

*While many of you have touched on the subject, what, if anything, can be done with the electronic information world (e.g., e-mail, WEB, cyberspace) to assist us in collaborating? And, are we the "natural" ones to collect archival materials (when they no longer have commercial value)?*

*As we come to the end of our second week of online discussion, I also wanted to be sure to get your thoughts on CRL's role in collaboration. What role would you like to see CRL play at this juncture? What needs should CRL address? Should it be more active or passive in pushing a national/international agenda? Thanks.*

[SB:]

*In my opinion, CRL should become something like the British Library Document Supply Centre and be a fulcrum in the transition of scientific/technical information from the subscription system to the free market. There needs to be some institution which can serve as coordinator in the construction of the new scientific/technical information system in a way that is both rational from the viewpoint of economics and preserves the heritage of human knowledge through proper archival management. With the scientific/technical information system properly restructured, individual libraries may again have resources to build unique collections and serve all constituent interests.*

Geoff Smith, Head of Modern Collections at the British Library, joined in from across the Atlantic:

[GS:]
*Colleagues*

Greetings from Britain. I'd hoped to join the discussion earlier but things have been hectic in the aftermath of the successful opening of the new British Library building

Steve Bensman's comment that 'anybody going into collection development is a fool' struck a chord. After a year in a new post as Head of Modern Collections at the British Library, with responsibilities to look at Library wide collection development policy and cooperation issues, I can understand why some might think so. I'm not sure I see my taking on the job as folly, but I've found collection development to raise issues more complex than any other areas of professional activity I've been involved in.

I still (foolishly?) have a basic sense that cooperation can work, at least in some areas of library activity. I was previously Head of the BL's Newspaper Library, heavily involved in NEWSPLAN, a cooperative project for the identification, listing, preservation and provision of access to British and Irish local newspapers. The project is similar to the US Newspaper Program, and the success of both makes me believe that cooperation can be successful where there is sense of common purpose, a clearly defined set of material (even on a large scale) with an evident need for action, and an acceptance by the outside world that the enterprise is worthwhile. However it also depends on being able to make strong cases for funding, whether from external sources or from the institutions participating, and, crucially, the funding sources themselves having the necessary money.

I was talking yesterday to a colleague from The Netherlands. She is collection development coordinator for the Royal Library (the Dutch National Library) and has a de-facto role to lead coordination and cooperation on collection development in The Netherlands. All of the major academic libraries work together with the Royal Library on collection development and access issues. Each library has a coordinator and there is a committee which brings together all of the coordinators and meets regularly to discuss and agree matters of mutual concern.

All of the libraries use the same computer system (Pica); with this they are able to see the holdings and on order records of the other libraries to help their selection decisions. There is a common file of proposed serials cancellations so that they can identify and where *possible prevent the cancellation of unique/last copy titles within The Netherlands. They have adopted a common classification system and are using this together with the Conspectus methodology to carry out collection assessments.*

*They cooperate on reference and borrowing access, interlending and document supply so that library users within the system can get access to the holdings of the whole system. Students even have free travel tickets to go use other collections if their own institution does not have the material they want!*

*It helps that both the Royal Library and the academic libraries are primarily funded by the same parent body, the Department of Education.*

*So: co-operation on collection development can work. The contact for any further information on the Dutch experience is Trix Bakker at the Koninklijke Bibliotheek in The Hague (trix.bakker@konbib.nl).*

*UK experience on cooperation is more fragmentary and complex. There has long been cooperation in the public library sector on interlending and on subject specialization schemes. In the academic and specialist sectors there has been cooperation and coordination on collection development and access within particular disciplines. For research level material, particularly serials, there has traditionally been consensus that the British Library's Document Supply Centre has been effective in providing systematic collecting and access, offering a centralized copying and interlending service based on its own extensive collections, with agreed back up arrangements with other libraries for material it does not hold.*

*There are now challenges to this centralized model both from the competition of alternative sources of supply for high-use material, electronic and paper-based, and from the exploration of cooperative alternatives to centralized document supply particularly within the university library sector. The revenue and budget challenges which arise may then threaten the breadth of collecting which validates the centralized model.*

*There is a growing acceptance of the need for a national UK strategy for library support for research through cooperative/distributed approaches. There is as yet no single forum for bringing together the relevant interested parties. The fact that the British Library is funded through the Department of Culture, and the universities through the Department of Education, with business interests channeled through* the Department of Trade means that there is no single political ownership of the issue.

My following of the debate that you have been involved in over the last two weeks has been reassuring in confirming that the issues around cooperation on collection development really are complex and that I have not been overlooking some simple solution and way forward that are obvious to colleagues elsewhere but not to me. (Though maybe the Dutch have shown it is easy, really, even if they do admit it has taken them fifteen years of discussion to get this far).

Thanks to CRL for letting me listen in, and to all of you for your ideas.-Yours in folly

[MW:]
Thanks so much for sharing your thoughts and concerns. It is reassuring on this end, as well, to know that the bundle of issues that we are dealing with have not found easy solution elsewhere.

While I am still so new to CRL that I don't yet feel I completely grasp the entire workings of the organization:-) I do think that more involvement of the membership at the daily level of collection building, managing, and bibliographic work (along the Dutch lines you mentioned) is necessary. Too often the people who do the actual work are represented by administrators (with good intentions even).

[GS:]
Thanks. Trix Bakker said that one of the reasons the cooperation was effective was that the coordinators were all involved in collection development–there was a separate high level steering group that picked up the politics.

[DJ:]
I agree with you, Milt, and have seen this in action, through what I consider to be successful cooperative collection development initiatives among area librarians at the level of the bibliographers. It does seem that once the issue becomes clouded with additional layers of bureaucracy and decision-making that it becomes more difficult to design/carry out a project–although, as Geoff says, sometimes the politics need to be handled by higher-ups. But the people who know and understand the field and the patterns of use and publication are in the best position to design realistic and yet effective projects. We've seen it via the area studies council of CRL, certainly.

As the allotted time for our online discussion was drawing to a close (not to mention the Christmas season counting down), I thought to stimulate things with a final volley, so to speak:

[MW:]
*Partners*:
*With all the diverse institutions which make up our library world, one would think that we would want to find some focal institution to represent our collaborative needs (those that are common to everyone). We have finally agreed, haven't we? that no one single institution can supply everything to its patrons from its own collection(s), so doesn't it make sense to explore every avenue of collaboration, partnership, etc.?*

*Since this online discussion ends this Sunday, I hope that some of you "lurkers" out there will join in with your thoughts before this is over.*

*Tomorrow is the final day for the online discussion. Anything you want to comment on? Is there really no way to organize beyond libraries of the same feather? Are the teaching faculty only reachable via "personal bibliographers?" Whither cooperation? down the commercial highways of passive reaction?*

A late lurker, E. Paige Weston, Library Systems Coordinator, Illinois Library Computer Systems Office, chimed in with:

[EPW:]
*Dear Partners*:
*While I've been waiting for a moment to compose a note, I've been watching for the Consortium Concerns thread. Was it woven in to a message I missed? If not, I'll guess I'll just have to spin it (and weave it?) myself. Here's some of what I worry about:*

*How does a consortium support office (like the one I work in) add value to a shared electronic collection? How do we facilitate electronic collections development across a whole consortium in a way that benefits the whole consortium, when member institutions do \*not\* share (and are not likely to share) their collection developers?*

*The Illinois Library Computer System Organization's (ILCSO's) Electronic Resources Committee charged itself with identifying electronic subscription opportunities when such will provide "benefits to the community in cost savings, user services, or system integration." So far this committee has acted without a written collection development policy for the consortium. Clearly such a document is needed,* and is finally being drafted. When adopted, this policy will help guide us, but here's what happens: many of our institutions have more than one consortial affiliation (some have three or more!). These libraries feel stymied (thwarted?) in their own collection development proceedings because

- they're reluctant to act alone, and forego potential cost savings that come from group discounts
- they're frustrated at the pace of consortial negotiations (librarians do everything by committee, and always want to reach consensus; vendors tend to deliberate longer when they're contracting with a consortium of 45 than when they're contracting with a single institution)
- they're *extremely* frustrated at the lack of coordination among consortia with overlapping membership: who springs for Britannica Online? who springs for PsycINFO? (Notice how no one ever says, "Phew, there's *way* too much communicating going on here!"?)

So, as I said, our consortial collection development policy is in development. Beyond this essential document, what are some good strategies for communication, cooperation, and success (measured as "benefits in cost savings, user services, or system integration") within, between, and *across* consortia?

I'd like to say Thanks to the host: Milton, it's been a great party. I'm sorry I've had to be a wallflower for so much of it. I'll be thinking about what I've "heard" (and will continue to hear, I hope) at this party for many months to come.

[DS:]
*Paige,*

You raise an issue that is very important to me. I have thought a lot about it and have no easy solutions, especially as consortia proliferate and expand the problem. Part of my vision for CRL's future is for it to seek to coordinate the major storage and repository libraries to do just what you suggest: reduce ambiguity and redundance. It is possible that CRL could extend that role to include broader coordination and communication among the consortia. Competition among consortia is a barrier and that is a very different role than CRL has ever conceived. Still!?

At this point it seemed time to bring our "experimental chat" to a close, but not without several fond farewells and "until we meet agains" to pick up the ongoing conversation:

[MW:]
*Paige,*

*Thanks for your comments. Often we are not sure what we are going to do until we share our problems and ideas. This online discussion has given me plenty of food for thought–and some partners to continue the dialogue. Thanks.*

[DJ]
*Milt et al.,*

*I feel a sense of "unfinished business" in our discussion, and I suspect it is because I (we?) don't have the time and/or peace of mind at this time of year (trying to wrap things up before the holidays, prepare for Midwinter, etc.) to consider the many questions the discussion has raised and to respond thoughtfully. I am not sure what the answer is, other than to prolong the discussion or open another "chapter" at a later date.*

[MW:]
*Deborah,*

*Agree with you. I think another chapter at a later date seems reasonable. Many thanks to all of you who helped launch this. I believe that such an online discussion could become a special feature of CRL. We will look into it. In the meantime, HAPPY HOLIDAYS and KEEP THE CONTENT!*

[DH:]
*I agree with Deborah that our discussion(s) have very much of an unfinished feel to them–and also that this has been a tough time of year to focus in on the exchange. I can imagine some sort of summary of the threads and topics we've raised to date as a jumping-off point for renewed exchanges in the New Year. A continued discussion might allow us both to bring some of our themes closer to closure (or even coherence), and to knit them together into a bigger picture of where cooperation is now, and where it might be headed. Thanks.*

[MW:]
*Dan (et al.),*

*We will pick this up again in the future for all the reasons that you and others have suggested. I will also monitor this online site until the day before Christmas for any of you who want to chime in until then. Best*

[BA:]
*Greetings, all:*
*I agree with much that has been said on this list, but I especially agree that we should take a bit of time to finish the discussion. I'm game to participate again, Milt, if you are brave enough to take this on after ALA.*

And so our virtual conversation ended, as it began, with lots of thoughtful questions, ideas and concerns. There was more to do, certainly; after all, we are building the world's best Research Library!

# Index

Academic Research and Library Resources: Changing Patterns in America (Osburn), 4-5
Access, local and global collections, 15-16
Allen, Barbara McFadden, 60-65, 63-65
Atkinson, Ross, 13

Baker, Nicholson, 9
Bakker, Trix, 88-89
Bensman, Stephen J., 60,62-63,65-66, 73,75-77,78,80,84-85,86
Bibliographers, 30,64-65,71-73
Book publishing, annual, 4
British Library Document Supply Centre, 15,77,78,88

Canadian Institute for Scientific and Technical Information (CISTI), 15
CARL Uncover, 15
Center for Research Libraries (CRL), 5,24,87
　accomplishments of, 51-52
　contributions to cooperative collection development, 50-51
　cooperative collection development and, 52-53
　cooperative collection development and, 42-43
　current operations, 53
　future cooperative collection development initiatives of, 43-44
　future role in cooperative collection development, 54-57

　reasons for establishing, 47-50
Collection development, 4-5. *See also* Cooperative collection development
　changing nature of, 41-42
Collection management
　current trends and practices, 6-11
　formative years (1950-1985), 2-6
　major tasks of, 5
　U.S. trends in, 11-15
Collection management librarians, 11
Committee for Institutional Cooperation Virtual Catalog, 40
Consortiums, 90-91
Cooperative collection development. *See also* Collection development
　assumptions of, in pre-Internet era, 22-27
　budgetary implications, 40-41
　concerns about, 27-29
　CRL and, 42-43
　CRL's characteristics for, 52-53
　CRL's contributions to, 50-51
　difficulty of, 61-62
　difficulty of implementing, 25-27
　digitization and, 31
　early attempts, 5-6
　environment for, 38-39
　forms of formal activities in, 24
　future initiatives by CRL in, 43-44
　future of, 33-35
　Internet era of, 29-33
　issues in, 38
　national/international aspects, 64
　options in, 62-63
　scientific/technical journals and, 65-66
　selection and, 80-81
　United Kingdom experience, 87-89

© 1998 by The Haworth Press, Inc. All rights reserved.

CRL. *See* Center for Research Libraries (CRL)

Digital information systems, 9-11
Digitization, 31
Document delivery, 14,63-64,75,76-77

Electronic collection development, 90-91
Electronic information, 41
Electronic information systems, 9-11
Electronic journals, 12-13
E-mail, 30
E-Print Archive, 12

Fall, John, 49
Farmington Plan, 5,37
First-copy costs, 83,84-85
Free market, 76-78

Ginsparg, Paul, 12
Global collections, managing local access to, 15-16

Hazen, Dan, 60,67-70,82-83
High Wire Press (Stanford University), 12-13
Holley, Edward, 3
Holley, Robert P., 19-22

Illinois Library Computer System Organization (ILCSO), 90
Information
 creating free markets for, 76
 electronic, 41
 explosion of, 2,4
 monopoly, 78
 rising cost of, 75-76

Information Access Company (IAC), 12
Information service vendors, 12
Information systems, library, 9-11
Institute for Scientific Information (ISI), 12,15
Interlibrary loan, 15,40
 inadequacy of speed, 62
Internet
 collecting all information myth and, 33
 cooperative collection development and, 29-33
 effect on traditional library materials, 31-33
 on-line catalogs and, 39-40

Jakubs, Deborah L., 60,61-62,71-75, 77-78,89-90
Journals, electronic, 12-13

Kent, Allen, 4

Librarians, insecurity of, 74-75
Linda Hall Library, 15
Local access, managing, and global collections, 15-18

Metcalf, Keyes D., 49
Monopoly power, 78
Mosher, Paul, 3-4,5

National Periodicals Center, 5

OhioLINK, 40,42-43
On-line catalogs, 39-40
Online Computer Library Center (OCLC), 12
On-line journals, 12-13
Osburn, Charles, 4-5
Ovid, 12

Print collections, loss of supremacy of, 13-15
Print information systems, 9-11
Project Muse (Johns Hopkins University), 12
Provision centers, 14
   creation of, 15

Rabe, Susan, 38,60,80-81
Reed Elsevier, 12
Research libraries
   change and, 11
   digital information services, 9-11
   economic decline of, 6-9
   effect of Internet on, 33-34
   post WWII expansion of, 3-4
   print resources in, 10-11
Research Libraries Group (RLG), 5, 12,37
Research Triangle Libraries, 5-6

Scholarly communication, changing structure of, 12
Scientific/technical journals, 75-76
   cooperative collection development and, 65-66

Selection, 80-81
Simpson, Don, 61,83-86,91-92
Smith, Geoff, 61,86-89
Subscription system, 76,86

University Microfilms International (UMI), 12
University of Minnesota Library, 10-11
*Use of Library Materials: The University of Pittsburgh Study* (Kent), 4

Wells, GladysAnn, 61,79-80
Weston, E. Paige, 61,90-92
Wilder, Stanley, 61,65-66
Wolf, Milton T., 61,70-72,74-75,77,79, 81-82, 90

For Product Safety Concerns and Information please contact our EU representative  GPSR@taylorandfrancis.com
Taylor & Francis Verlag GmbH, Kaufingerstraße 24, 80331 München, Germany